chic living with feng shui

Stylish Designs for Harmonious Living

Sharon Stasney

Main Street
A division of Sterling Publishing Co., Inc.
New York

Library of Congress Cataloging-in-Publication Data Available

10 9 8 7 6 5 4 3 2

This material was excerpted from the following
Sterling/Chapelle titles:
Feng Shui Chic, © 2000 by Sharon Stasney
Feng Shui Living, © 2003 by Sharon Stasney

Published by Sterling Publishing Co., Inc.
387 Park Avenue South, New York, NY 10016
© 2004 by Sterling Publishing Co., Inc.
Distributed in Canada by Sterling Publishing
c/o Canadian Manda Group, 165 Dufferin Street, Toronto,
Ontario, Canada M6K 3H6
Distributed in Great Britain by Chrysalis Books Group PLC
The Chrysalis Building, Bramley Road, London W10 6SP, England
Distributed in Australia by Capricorn Link (Australia) Pty. Ltd.
P.O. Box 704, Windsor, NSW 2756, Australia

Printed in China
All rights reserved

ISBN 1-4027-1745-8

For information about custom editions, special sales, premium
and corporate purchases, please contact Sterling Special Sales
Department at 800-805-5489 or specialsales@sterlingpub.com

Table of Contents

Introduction

Feng shui (pronounced fung schway) is thousands of years old, yet it is also today's latest design trend. Feng shui design is just as effective today as it was in Royal China because it is based on fundamental principles of how to create different energy states in the human body.

Every design choice generates a physical and emotional response in your body. Your choices can encourage you to slow down, relax, get creative, express enthusiasm, feel grounded and secure—whatever you need from your space. You do not need to incorporate Asian decor items to benefit from feng shui. Whatever your decorating style, feng shui principles will help you design a home you want to live in.

Applying feng shui principles to your home can:
▲ Open you to new experiences.
▲ Enhance relaxation/rejuvenation.
▲ Stabilize your moods.
▲ Encourage creativity/confidence in family.
▲ Encourage focus on detailed tasks.
▲ Increase intimacy in your relationships.
▲ Strengthen immune system/energy levels.
▲ Help you let go of unwanted clutter.
▲ Bring balance/harmony into your home/life.

How it all works

Your relationship to home

Your home is a powerful force in your life. Every day it offers a greater understanding of who you are and what your life is currently focused on. Your relationships with abundance, health, intimacy, creativity, and family are mirrored on your walls, ingrained in your tables, and reflected in your pictures. Home is where you physically manifest your beliefs about the world.

However, home is more than just a mirror; it is a dynamic force that is constantly responding to the intentions of those who live in it. Your home affects you just as you affect it. The colors, patterns, and structures with which you surround yourself generate energetic vibrations that may or may not serve you. A depressed person, for example, might create a home in which everything is low to the ground, dark, and slow-moving. Such an environment, besides being a reflection of the person's mental and emotional state, will physically re-create depressed states in a person's body every day. The good news is that changing the decor of the home could change a person's energy in a healing way. Physically shifting elements in your space shifts the way energy flows through your body.

Your home is an active force in your life, regardless of whether or not you attend to it. By becoming aware of how your home mirrors you, and how to shift its energy, you can turn your home into a force that heals, restores balance, and encourages growth. Feng shui is the art of consciously making design choices that support your life's path.

Integrating feng shui in your own way

You can integrate feng shui into your design choices on many different levels, depending on what resonates with you. Each design choice has a physical aspect (the color blue relaxes the muscles and can lower your heart rate and blood pressure), a psychological/emotional aspect (the color blue might depress you), a cultural aspect (bright blue doors are considered cheerful in Sante Fe but obnoxious in Boston).

Many traditional feng shui adjustments originate in a cultural and symbolic system (Royal China) that may not work for you. Once you understand the intent of each adjustment, you can modify the traditional adjustments to match your own cultural and personal symbolic system.

This book will explain the energetic intent of feng shui adjustments and provide guidance on implementing adjustments that work on multiple levels simultaneously. It is important to use only those adjustments that make sense to you and resonate with your intention for your home. Placing something in your home that you don't like just because it is "good feng shui" will not enhance your home or support your personal growth.

Chi

Feng shui design is based on the awareness that an electromagnetic energy flows around and through your body, linking you to every other person, object, and force in the universe.

Chi is the Chinese term for this universal life force that reminds us of the underlying connected nature of all things. You feel this energetic connection to others when someone walks into the room behind you and you feel the presence without turning around. Or perhaps you have walked into a room where two people are arguing. Even if they fall silent, the energy of their angry words hangs in the air. Sometimes this heavy chi can remain for days if it is not cleared.

Chi moves and changes form constantly. The chi in a human body transfers to the external environment and vice versa. Imagine sitting in a leather chair on a cold winter day. The chair is cold and does not radiate energy. After you sit in the chair for a while though, the heat energy from your body is transferred to the chair and the chair begins to give it back to you.

Chic Living with Feng Shui will provide exercises and opportunities for exploring how chi feels in your body (personal chi) and how radically your personal chi changes based on environment. After you make feng shui adjustments, you can measure the effectiveness in a meaningful way.

The energy field surrounding the body is called the aura.

Your aura

Personal chi is the interface between your body's energy and the environment's energy. Personal chi is often referred to as the "aura." The size and shape of your aura change constantly. Generally, you extend your aura when you feel comfortable, safe, or happy. This makes you seem more approachable to others.

Fearful, unhappy, or discomforting states typically cause you to retract your auric field, pull it in closer around you. The sensation known as "withdrawal" happens when you retract your energy so that your auric field no longer overlaps the other person's field. They feel the withdrawal of your personal chi.

You are constantly expanding and contracting your aura due to interpersonal and environmental triggers. Feng shui will help you be more aware of how your physical environment influences your aura.

As you sit reading *Chic Living with Feng Shui*, extend your awareness to the energy surrounding your body. How comfortable are you sitting in your chair? Do you feel supported? Protected? Comfortable? Get a sense of how far around you your energy extends. Now, pick up your chair (if it is one you can lift) and set it right in the middle of a doorway. As you now sit in the chair notice how your aura changes. Did you extend it further, indicating a greater sense of comfort and safety, or did you contract it? Obviously the size and type of chair will also make a difference in how you feel sitting in it. With feng shui, you realize that everything from position to color, to shape, to texture, effects your energy.

Flowers, bricks, wood, rocks—every organic force has chi.

Feeling energy move between your hands helps you experience energy, rather than just read about it.

1. Hold the rods loosely around the base, so they swing freely. Keep hands about shoulder-width apart, parallel to the floor. Tell the rods (either mentally or out loud) to go straight ahead. This grounds your own energy field, sending it down into the earth and helps you become more neutral. Instead of picking up shifts in your energy, the rods can now measure the shifts in the environment.

2. Once you find a neutral position, you can ask yes or no questions. When you think "yes," the rods will cross in front, when you think "no," they will spread out.

Feeling chi between your hands

A starting point in working with energy is to feel the chi between your hands. The palms have chakras (places in the body where chi concentrates), and it is often easier to feel energy there.

Stand with your feet shoulder-width apart, elbows bent, hands parallel with the floor facing each other. Clench your hands into fists a couple of times to get the blood flowing to that part of your body. Then raise your hands to shoulder height, spreading them out further than your shoulders, and slowly start to bring them together. It helps to visualize holding a round ball of energy between your hands. As you bring them closer, you will begin to feel a tingling sensation between your hands, especially at the fingertips.

As you continue to push this energy in and pull it back out again (without letting your hands touch), it starts to feel like strong magnets are pulling your hands together whenever they get close.

Using dowsing rods to measure chi

Another way to measure shifts in chi is to use dowsing rods. Dowsers have used these L-shaped rods for centuries to find water and pockets of geopathic stress. (Geopathic stress pockets occur when intense volatile energies under the earth's crust bubble up to the surface, creating areas where the energy is not healthy for human beings.)

You can use dowsing rods to find the edge of an energy field, see where chi builds up in your space, or understand your own energetic response to different placements. Dowsing rods are helpful because they help you visually perceive shifts in your personal chi. The more senses you activate in understanding chi, the more energy work becomes a part of your reality.

3. To use the rods to locate shifts in energy, walk slowly through your space watching where the rods spread apart.

If you have someone with you, use the rods to measure the size of his aura and see what happens when he stands in different positions. Holding the rods in front of you in the neutral position, walk very slowly toward the person. When the rods hit the edge of the person's auric field, they will spread out.

Now have the person turn around so his back is to you and walk toward him again. Notice how much smaller his aura is when his back is turned to you. This is because he pulls his aura in tighter around his body to protect himself when he's in a vulnerable position.

You can use dowsing rods to gauge the impact of your environment on your chi as well. Stand against a solid wall and have your friend hold the rods to measure the edge of your aura. Now stand in front of a sharp edge, such as the edge of a table, or a sharp corner where two walls come together. Notice what happens to your aura.

When walking into the path of a mirror, dowsing rods typically spread out. This is because a mirror activates the surrounding area. Place seating to the side of a mirror, rather than directly in front to avoid the strong chi flow of the mirror.

Chi & the chakras

The chakra system is the Vedic system of understanding how energy flows in the body. A chakra is a place in the body where energy concentrates. The seven major chakras are located starting at the base of the spine and running up the spine to the crown of the head.

First chakra

The first chakra is referred to as the root chakra and is located at the base of the spine. It governs our fight/flight mechanism and is primarily concerned with safety, tribal support, and our place in the physical world. The color of the root chakra is red, preferably a deep maroon and deep earthy browns. It aligns with the element of earth in feng shui five-element theory.

Second chakra

The second chakra is located in the reproductive organs. It governs sexuality, interactions with another being, our sense of a social self, our attachments to money, and our need to "control" others, ourselves, or situations. Its color is primarily orange, but it is also associated with pink. It aligns with water in five-element theory.

Third chakra

The third chakra is your center of personal power. It is your source of willpower and influence. It is located in the solar plexus (the stomach/rib area). When someone takes a jab at you (physically or emotionally) you feel a sharp intake of energy in your stomach. When your third chakra energy is weak, you experience the phenomena of butterflies in your stomach. This airy, spinning sensation makes it difficult to assert yourself or present yourself in a forceful way. It is usually harder to stand up for your rights or feel a strong sense of self-esteem if your third chakra is weak. Its color is yellow. It aligns itself with fire in five-element theory.

Fourth chakra

The fourth chakra is the heart center, the source of unconditional love and compassion for others, and the ability to forgive and let go of grievances. This chakra is the central point that balances the energies of the lower three chakras, which are concerned with the well-being of the individual, and with the higher three chakras, which are more cosmic and universal in nature. It is the center of healing energies, healing both body and spirit. Its color is green and its physical location in the body is the heart space. It aligns itself with earth in five-element theory.

Fifth chakra

The fifth chakra is the voice chakra, located at the throat. It is the center of shifting from a personal power base to a spiritual one. The energy of the fifth chakra opens your connection to a guiding force beyond your personal means. You move from thinking that you have to do it all to aligning yourself with this guiding power, whatever form that power takes for you. The ability to trust a guiding power always comes from feeling the healing love of the universe, therefore, the fifth chakra follows the fourth. Someone with strong fifth chakra energy is able to let go of personal attachments and open up to a more universal sense of self. Its color is blue. It aligns itself with wood in five-element theory.

There are many books explaining how energy moves through the chakras. *Chic Living with Feng Shui* uses this system to explain how different feng shui adjustments affect different parts of the body, which in turn affect different life aspects. The basic associations between the major seven chakras, body locations, and life aspects are included below.

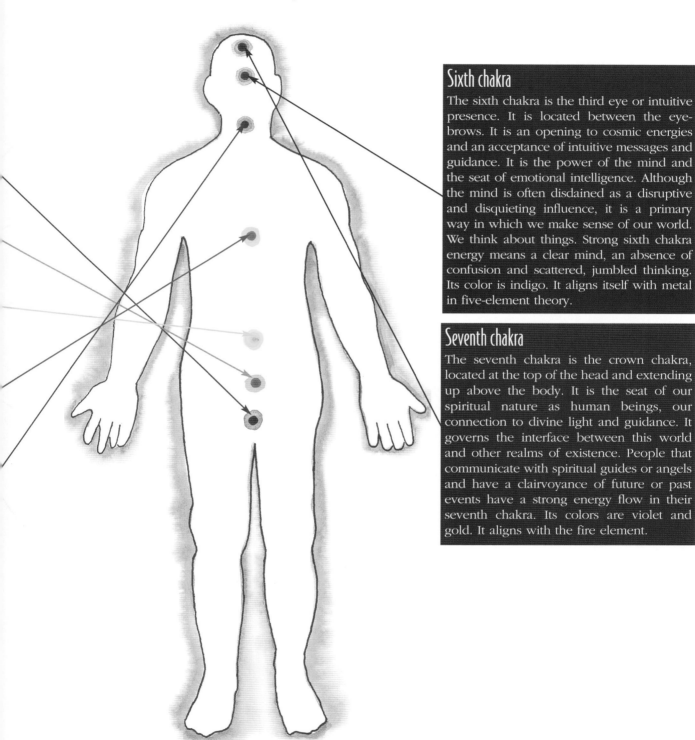

Sixth chakra

The sixth chakra is the third eye or intuitive presence. It is located between the eyebrows. It is an opening to cosmic energies and an acceptance of intuitive messages and guidance. It is the power of the mind and the seat of emotional intelligence. Although the mind is often disdained as a disruptive and disquieting influence, it is a primary way in which we make sense of our world. We think about things. Strong sixth chakra energy means a clear mind, an absence of confusion and scattered, jumbled thinking. Its color is indigo. It aligns itself with metal in five-element theory.

Seventh chakra

The seventh chakra is the crown chakra, located at the top of the head and extending up above the body. It is the seat of our spiritual nature as human beings, our connection to divine light and guidance. It governs the interface between this world and other realms of existence. People that communicate with spiritual guides or angels and have a clairvoyance of future or past events have a strong energy flow in their seventh chakra. Its colors are violet and gold. It aligns with the fire element.

12

Yin & yang in balance

The chi that flows through the earth, the heavens, and your body, moves in two general forms. We describe these forms of movement as yin and yang, the receptive and the creative.

The yin/yang dichotomy divides energy into opposites that attract each other. This attraction creates movement. We need to balance this interaction between yin and yang to keep energy flowing at the right pace in our lives.

Too much yin energy, and movement slows, chi stagnates, the body shuts down, and ill health results. Too much yang, and chi speeds along too quickly, life changes rapidly, and one's blood pressure and heart rate rise, again resulting in ill health.

When designing your home, balancing these two forces can return you to a state of balance and wholeness. Shifting the yin/yang balance of your home can generate physical, mental, and emotional healing.

Before you start moving furniture around, however, it is important to first ascertain whether the people living in the home have a stronger yin or a stronger yang force in their bodies. Based on this assessment, you can balance the environment and the body.

In this room the black furniture (yin) balances the yang force of the yellow walls. The upward-reaching plants and corner light bring energy up while the heavy square fireplace adds stability, keeping all in balance.

Personal chi assessment

No one is entirely yin or yang, but at any given point in time you have a predominant energy in your body. You will notice that this energy shifts with the seasons, the time of day, or even food choices. This is important because what you need from your home will change according to seasons, times of day, and moods. As your body shifts, so must your space. Start with how you are feeling today. Check the attributes in each list below that describe you in the present moment and count up the score. Once you tally your yin and yang attributes, you will have a pretty good idea of where you fit in the spectrum.

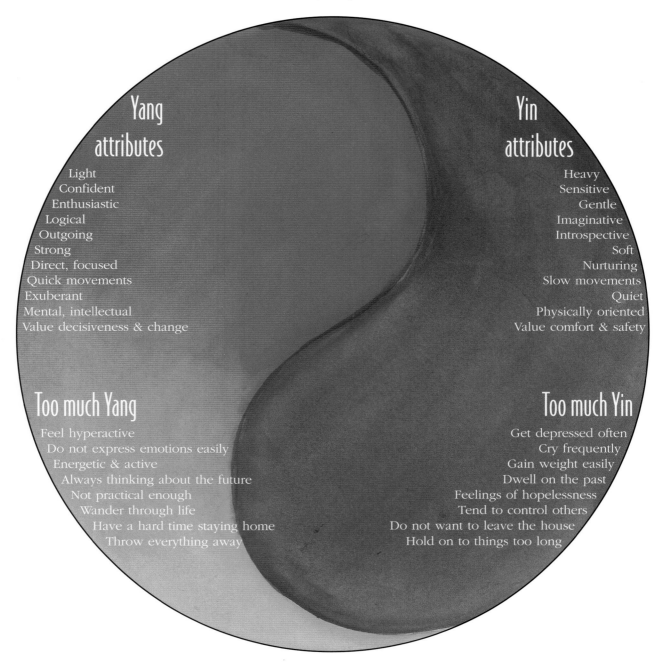

Yang attributes

Light
Confident
Enthusiastic
Logical
Outgoing
Strong
Direct, focused
Quick movements
Exuberant
Mental, intellectual
Value decisiveness & change

Yin attributes

Heavy
Sensitive
Gentle
Imaginative
Introspective
Soft
Nurturing
Slow movements
Quiet
Physically oriented
Value comfort & safety

Too much Yang

Feel hyperactive
Do not express emotions easily
Energetic & active
Always thinking about the future
Not practical enough
Wander through life
Have a hard time staying home
Throw everything away

Too much Yin

Get depressed often
Cry frequently
Gain weight easily
Dwell on the past
Feelings of hopelessness
Tend to control others
Do not want to leave the house
Hold on to things too long

Yin decor adjustments

Shapes

Include curved or flowing shapes. Exchanging a sturdy wood coffee table for a curvy wicker one will shift the balance from yang to yin. Build-in slopes, terraces, or cascading effects with garden beds, curtains, or candles. The circle is an exception; although it is curved, it spins energy outward and is, therefore, yang.

Colors

Tone it down. Deep dark colors, muddy tones (brick red, sage green), soft pastels, and muted hues all increase yin energy in the home. Black is the most yin color of all, pulling energy inward. Stay away from sharp white walls and bouncy yellow if you want to increase yin energy.

Furnishings

Soften & absorb. Although mirrors make great feng shui cures, too many mirrors create an intensely yang space. Swap wood furniture for upholstered versions, get rid of the metal table base with the round glass top, add paper screens and large cushions, cover the table with a cloth. Another way to create a yin vibration is to choose furniture and decor items that are low to the ground. Hanging pictures lower than eye level will also move energy down.

Lighting

Think soft. Soften overhead lights by installing dimmer switches. Get full window coverings. Increase yin by adding hanging lamps and downward lamp lighting.

Windows & floor treatments

Rich & full. Rich textures slow down the chi flow. For windows, move from wood shutters to drapes, or from metal mini blinds to folded roman shades. For flooring, cover that tile floor or marble entryway with thick rugs or rush matting. And remember, wood floors are nice, but a plush carpet softens an agitated mind and absorbs excess stress.

Density & size

Fill it up. The more furniture you fit into a space, the denser and more yin the space becomes. If you need more stability, you can anchor a room with large, heavy items such as an armoire, a chest, or a buffet. In the kitchen, anchor light-colored countertops by placing something heavy such as pottery or a potted plant in the corners.

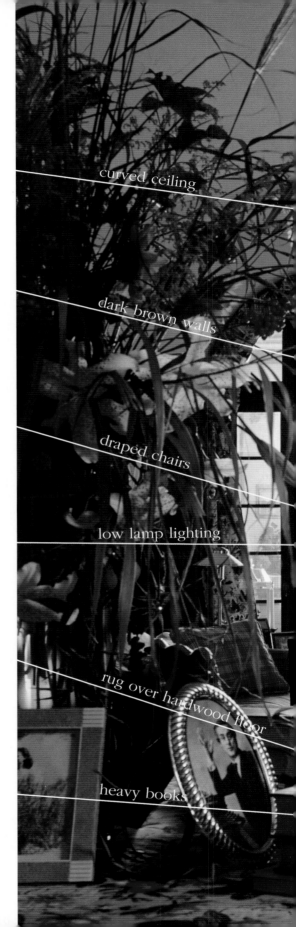

curved ceiling

dark brown walls

draped chairs

low lamp lighting

rug over hardwood floor

heavy books

Yang decor adjustments

Shapes

Straighten up. A straight vertical line will remind you to stand up for yourself and ask for what you want. Triangles and pyramids are dynamic and motivating, helping us push past boundaries that no longer serve.

Colors

Turn on the heat. Color is a great way to shift a space that is too yin to one that is just right, but chances are, if you are holding a lot of yin energy in your body, you will be fearful of including bright colors in your space. Start small. Put a bright red teapot on your stove. Buy a set of deep plum sheets. Float tangerine orange and Mediterranean blue candles in your bath.

Furnishings

Be firm. No slouchy couch for you. Opt for one with wooden arms and a firm seat. Use mirrors, glass, and polished stone. Be certain to replace hanging plants with plants that point upward and hang pictures higher than eye level. Remove items that sit directly on the floor, such as baskets, books, magazine racks, or knickknacks.

Lighting

Go natural. Bright lights can enhance your mood in addition to your walls. If at all possible, use natural light. Natural light includes the full spectrum of color vibrations for a balanced emotional and physical impact. Our favorite rooms are usually those that have natural light on two sides, because the proportion of natural light to artificial light is 50 percent or more. If you do have a room with a single window, consider the possibility of putting in another window (it is less expensive than you think to have a wall made into a window). If you cannot work with the walls, add skylights.

When adding natural light is not possible, take off the window coverings, add a row of track lighting, and install lights under counters. Go for overhead lighting rather than lamps, use halogens that send light upward instead of downward pointing lamps.

Windows & floor treatments

Think open & clean. Fluffy and soft is not what you are after. Remove curtains or replace with wooden blinds. Opt for vertical blinds, rather than horizontal treatments. Allow marble, tile, and hardwood floors to lend you strength and provide the assurance of a stable foundation. Make certain surfaces are smooth and glossy to speed up chi flow and pull you out of an emotional mire.

Density & size

Lighten up. Too many furnishings can weigh you down, create stagnant chi, and make it hard to get moving. Make certain pathways between furniture items are at least three feet wide, preferably four. Use furnishings that are lighter in weight and smaller in stature, such as items made from wicker or bamboo. In the kitchen, clear off counters and streamline appliances.

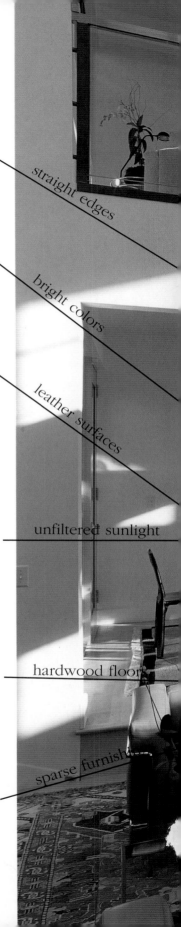

straight edges

bright colors

leather surfaces

unfiltered sunlight

hardwood floor

sparse furnish

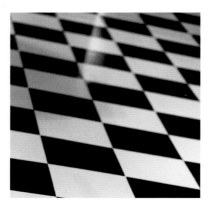

What do you need from your environment?

Your body and your environment are constantly exchanging energy. Your physical environment affects the energy in your body and the emotions and electromagnetic charge in your body leave their imprint on your environment. Once you have an idea of whether you carry more yin or yang in your body, you can work with this dance of energy to create more balance in your life. If you hold a lot of yin in your body, increase the amount of yang in your environment. If you hold too much yang, add yin energy in your home.

Let's say you are choosing flooring for a home office. Assume you have a naturally high energy level and are having a hard time focusing in the office. The house has an open floor plan with lots of windows and light-colored furnishings. If you choose hardwood flooring, shiny tile, or vinyl, it will speed up energy and make it even more difficult for you to concentrate. If you choose a thick textured carpet in a muted hue, it will slow down the energy in the room, help you anchor (ground) the energy in your body so that you can channel that energy into your work.

Note: This is not always a case of choosing what feels natural to you. If you tend to have a predominance of yin in your body, design choices that feel natural (in kin with your nature) will have a strong yin force as well. Although we often intuitively balance out a strong yin by bringing in more yang and vice versa, sometimes you need to consciously work with this balance. The more out of balance the body is, the less it will crave what it really needs. In this case, take inventory of how each item that you bring into your space shifts the yin/yang balance. Do not add too much too fast or you will begin to feel like you are living in a stranger's house.

Understanding the elements

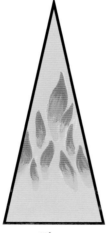

Fire:
expansion &
transformation

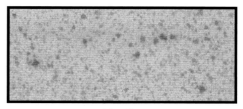

Earth:
grounding & support

Wood:
personal growth

When considering your space in terms of energy, the flow between yin and yang forces is a good place to start. You begin to view design choices according to how they move energy: whether it expands or contracts, moves higher or lower, speeds up or slows down. The five elements in feng shui explain how yin and yang manifest in five primary energy patterns. When you use the five elements to balance your environment, this balancing works inward and you feel it in your body. You might just notice that you are inclined to relax more in one room than another or that certain spaces invite you to stay longer than others.

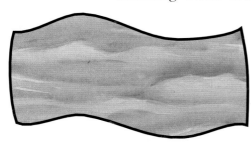

Water:
release & renewal

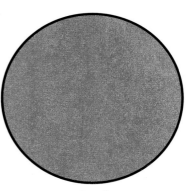

Metal:
mental power

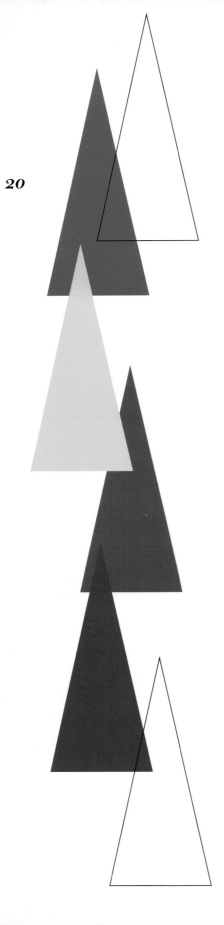

Fire: expansion & transformation

Fire is the power of transformation. Lots of fire energy in a home encourages lots of changes in the lives of those who live there. Fire energy helps you expand, open up to new ideas and ways of being. It gives you the push to share your gifts with the world.

Fire colors

You can increase the amount of fire energy in your home by the colors you choose. Although red and orange are traditionally associated with a fire vibration, any bright color will achieve the same energetic effect. What you are looking for is a certain dynamism, an active color that bounces light and energy.

The type of paint finish you choose also effects how much light energy is in the room. A semigloss will create a more reflective surface than a flat or a satin finish and will keep the light moving, increasing the energy in the room. High-gloss trim is a great way to add punch to a room. If your goal is to slow the energy down, however, consider using satin, eggshell, or flat finishes instead of semigloss, and avoid high-gloss trim.

Increase the amount of fire energy in your home through color, such as these bright yellow walls accented by the red standing clock. The triangular shapes throughout this room also increase fire energy.

Fire shapes & structures

Shapes and structures affect the energy of a room just as much as color. Shapes that generate fire energy are triangles (straight up or inverted), pyramids, diamonds, and sunbursts. These shapes send energy up and out and keep things moving.

Triangles represent the union of heaven, earth, and human. Triad energy is always volatile and fast moving. The straight lines and sharp angles keep energy speeding along, and change is inevitable. This is a good shape to use if you want to shake things up or bring change to a certain area of your life.

If you are drawn to triangles in your decorating, there is a reason why that fast, changing energy feels good to you. Think about what it is in your life that you may want to change and consciously use triangles to represent that life aspect.

Pyramids represent eternal life and communion with the gods. Based on earth but directed towards heaven, a pyramid reminds us to honor our own divine nature and that, by honoring it, the mundane is transformed into the sacred.

Pyramids are more grounded and less volatile than triangles because of their solid base and three-dimensional quality. They will help you reach for something that you feel is beyond you or joyfully accept acknowledgment for the divine being that you are.

Diamonds are another way to bring energy into a room. Diamonds direct a downward-moving energy up and out. Known for their brilliance, they represent your ability to shine and radiate your life force out into the world.

Diamonds can be easily integrated into your design through tile work. Other ways to use diamonds include stained glass work, wallpaper, and windows. You can even transform a normal square window by adding a diamond stained-glass insert. Fiery colors in the stained glass will enhance the fire vibration even more.

Sunbursts shoot energy out in every direction. They symbolize the transformation that occurs every morning as the first rays of the sun shoot out over the tops of mountains, turning the stillness of night into the activity of day. Sunbursts also mark high noon, the sun in its full radiance. When you bring sunbursts into your home, you encourage recognition of your own radiance and the potential to transform any seemingly dark aspect of your life into light.

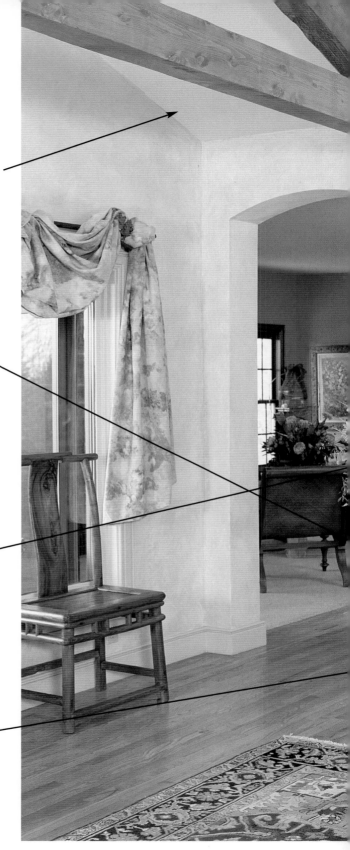

Fanning floral arrangements out at the top creates the expansive energy characteristic of fire.

To shift priorities to family and serenity, keep the television cabinet doors closed when not in use and use the fireplace often in season.

The diamond-shaped designs on these entertainment center doors keep energy moving in a vertical direction.

Design ideas for increasing fire

The lighter, brighter, and more reflective a room is, the more fire energy it holds. Paint walls semigloss instead of a satin finish, or paint trim a high gloss instead of a semigloss. Consider high-gloss picture frames instead of matte ones.

Increase the actual amount of lighting by adding spotlights, tea lights, lanterns, halogen lamps, or candles. Replace hanging plants with upward-shooting palms or yucca trees, and make certain they are planted in terra-cotta pots.

Pets are another way to increase fire vibration in your home. Even adding items that come from animals, such as feathers or leather, will increase fire.

Fireplace & television. There is a fundamental reason why homes with a fireplace sell faster than homes without. A fireplace echoes the days of the hearth, a sense of home, comfort, nurturing food, and good company.

Where a fireplace and a TV coexist, whichever object is more prominent will energetically and psychologically dominate the room. Shifting your relationship with your TV set, reducing its prominence by placing it behind closed doors, getting rid of a set, or moving it out of a prominent room, can reflect a shift in the prioritizing pattern of your life.

Cooking with fire. Fire energy burns away stagnation and returns the spirit. If you do not have a fireplace, use your stove. Notice how different it feels to use your stove instead of your microwave. Even if you are boiling water, lighting your stove (preferably a gas stove) generates an increase in personal chi, especially as it relates to overall health and the immune system.

Light on two sides. We require sunlight in order to survive—without it, our skin, mood, and overall health suffer. When people have a choice, they gravitate to rooms which have light on two sides, and leave the rooms which are lit only from one side unused and empty.

Natural light on only one side prevents chi from flowing smoothly from one side of the room to the other.

With natural light in on two sides of a room, the chi flow is balanced and draws energy across the room.

Earth: grounding & support

Earth energy is your grounding cord, your sense of safety, security, protection, and stability. It moves downward, holding things in place, making them stable and steady. Earth energy also moves slowly. It can manifest as dense, solid, heavy objects or as soft, comforting, nurturing objects. Either way, the effect is to become still, feel calm, and be at peace.

Earth energy reminds us that we live in a physical world with physical needs, and we need to honor the physical body. Earth elements with a lot of density ground the body as well as the spirit and help you feel your body's messages. The result of really listening to the body is balance and improved health.

When you do support yourself physically by buying the right chair or couch, that supportive energy ripples out into other aspects of your life. You begin to notice where you are not psychologically or emotionally supported and start to identify how you would like that support to manifest. You will feel more able to ask for support from your spouse, boss, and children when you learn to support your physical body by doing something as simple as choosing the right chair. You are taking an action that affirms in your psyche and spirit that you are worthy of and ready to accept supportive energy in your life.

Earth colors

Earth colors are muted rather than bright, dark rather than light, and grayed rather than clear. Browns and yellows are traditionally associated with earth energy, but be careful that the yellow is not a clear, bright yellow.

Earth colors slow chi down and help you center your energy lower in your body.

Earth shapes & structures

Earth structures provide stability and comfort. When made from earth materials such as brick, adobe, straw, or stone, the earth vibration in the structure increases exponentially.

Horizontal shapes encourage cohesion and connection. This energy flow is not concerned with growth as much as it is concerned with integration. Every home has a lot of horizontal shapes and structures such as tabletops, desks, beds, shelves, and ledges. What you do with these surfaces determines how strong the earth vibration is.

For example, if you cover your table with a cloth, perhaps even a thick velvet cloth, you increase the table's holding properties. If you put a glass top on your table, you decrease the table's ability to hold and slow energy. Make your choices according to your needs.

Horizontal patterns hold energy, vertical patterns keep it moving. You can use horizontal patterns to slow down a fast vertical chi flow.

Squares and rectangles used in your home express a desire for right action and integrity. Your living space becomes the foundation from which this right action moves out into the world. Rectangles are a particular form of the square which can either ground energy (if the longer side is horizontal) or move energy (if the longer side is vertical). Horizontal rectangles create a strong earth vibration. Switching from a tall dresser to a side-by-side, exchanging portrait pictures (vertical) for landscapes (horizontal), and choosing wide (horizontal) windows instead of tall (vertical) ones will all increase the grounding in your home.

Squares in the picture frame, coffee table, and fireplace bring in earth energy.

28

Replacing plastic pots for terra-cotta ones draws in earth energy.

Design ideas for increasing earth

You can create an earth vibration by increasing comfort or stability. You want your family and guests to feel as if they are wrapped up in a cozy blanket in mom's kitchen. A little clutter can actually be a good thing here, especially if things are placed low to the ground. A basket here, a ceramic rabbit there, will draw energy closer to the earth and increase the downward pull of the space.

Remove transitional items such as futons, which are used as a couch one minute and a bed the next. A bed with a

To increase safety and stability in a room, add heavy furniture such as armoires, buffets, or cabinets.

The built-in oven and refrigerator add to the stability of this room. Using organic materials such as the black granite in this countertop also increases earth energy.

To add earth energy, consider adding one or more of the following built-in items:

▲ Garbage disposal
▲ Spice rack
▲ Desk
▲ Bookshelves
▲ Window seat
▲ Telephone ledge
▲ Bunk beds
▲ Breakfast bench
▲ Ironing board
▲ Garage shelving
▲ Tool bench

Wall faux finishes

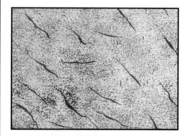

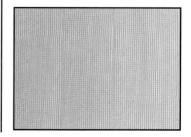

headboard and a regular couch will slow down change and increase the feeling in the room that life is stable, safe, and trustworthy.

Walls. Thin walls made from sheetrock or drywall do not have the ability to hold energy as thick walls do; they lack density. Brick or adobe walls bring a more stable, grounded feel. You can create this grounding visually through faux-painting, rag-rolling, or layering paint. Whether you create the look of marble, brick, or aged stone, the paint gives depth and density to a flat wall. You can also create thick walls by building into or on the wall itself. Built-in furniture pieces such as window seats or bookshelves give your wall and your home the energy of permanence.

Ceilings. What's modern, exciting, and trendy does not always serve the soul, and this definitely applies to ceiling height. Vaulted, slanted, or high ceilings lift energy up and keep it moving. Low ceilings also have their place in the home, especially in bedrooms. Because they hold energy in and help people close down over-active receptors, they increase feelings of stability, permanence, and safety.

If all your ceilings are 10 feet or more in height, you can visually lower the ceiling by choosing the right lighting fixture. Lighting fixtures that hang lower draw the energy of the ceiling down and achieve the same effect as a low ceiling.

Metal: mental power

Metal energy is the energy of the mind. Like the mind, it has two primary aspects—the left-brained, intellectual aspect and the right-brained, creative aspect. The left-brained aspect is dense, and its density serves as a magnet to draw scattered energies together to a physical center. It helps you focus and concentrate on intellectual tasks.

The right-brained aspect is dynamic; it pulls and pushes and spins, the natural result of many different energies coming together into a central location. Both forms pull energies together.

Metal colors

The feng shui colors for the left-brained metal vibration are white, silver, and gray. Many clients paint the interior of their houses white because they want a neutral feeling. This sharp edge can be helpful in some situations (an office for example) because it helps people focus on detailed tasks, such as computer programming or accounting. White walls in the more social rooms of your home, however, will not serve you well.

If you like the look of white walls, but do not want the sharp energy associated with them, opt for a creamy or rosy white. The creamy or rosy whites have an earth element as well as the metal, and soften the overall effect. You can also leave three of the walls white but paint one wall a soft warm color. This one wall will balance the rest of the room and take away the sharp edge.

The right-brained aspect of metal is represented by rainbow colors. Bringing all seven rainbow rays into your home, especially into your creative studio, can be a powerful boost to creativity. Rainbow rays are also healing to the body.

White is anything but neutral. It is intellectual energy, and too much of it can make people sharp and sarcastic, similar to the sharp edge of an ax.

Metal shapes & structures

The circle is a yang form of metal energy. When metal melts, it forms droplets or circles. In a circle, energy is dynamic, constantly moving, pushing, pulling, and expanding. This is the natural result of combining energy flows. Although the circle shape spins energy outward, it also draws energies together. The wrapping motion of the circle draws the energy from one side of the circle to the other side. This means that the circle pulls separate strands of energy into a unified force, which it then spins outward.

In psychological terms, the circle shape represents the merging of individual consciousness with the collective. "To sit in circles is to array ourselves in a living mandala of community, offering the experience of being one voice in a collective awareness or effort. Cutting through the isolation and fear which is so characteristic of our culture, group practices ride on the interplay between our identities as individuals and as a collective, preparing us to be community members." (Vishu Magee, *Archetypal Design*, p. 109)

When we use the circle or the arc in our design, we bring communal energies into our living spaces.

When you sit in a living room where the furniture is shaped to form a circle, notice how it draws the energies of everyone sitting there into relationship with each other. Anything circular, such as the fireplace and center table in this photograph, can hold the sacred energy of community once you make the connection.

34

Increase metal outside by adding metal wind chimes, planters, a mailbox, or even a weather vane.

Metal items in round shapes spark the playful, yang aspect of the metal element.

Shiny metal, like copper or brass, attracts more chi than dull metal.

Design ideas for increasing metal

Wind chimes and bells have long been used in many different meditation practices to call the mind back from its wanderings and return it to the present moment. They can be used to increase focus both inside and outside the house. Other metal objects such as tables, desks, shelves, or accessories can also boost the intellectual or creative energy in a room.

Even a wine cellar (typically a very earthy place) can have a strong metal element if you use metal and curves in the door.

The arc and the cut-away in this hallway are metal's more yin forms. They pull energy in towards a central point, condensing and focusing it. Yin metal energy increases concentration and intellectual focus. The strongest inward pull is at the inner angle or curve.

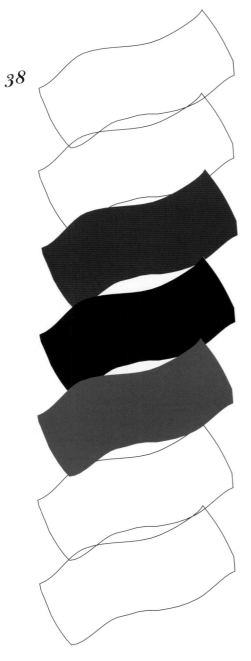

Water: release & renewal

Water energy has two aspects: still water and moving water. These vary greatly in their creation and their effect. Moving water (yang) moves energy from high to low, spreading out as it flows, equalizing the energy of all surrounding forces. It helps you release and let go of what no longer serves your best interests. It also represents the flow of money and abundance in your life.

Still water (yin) is a return to the womb. It settles, slows, and calms the energies surrounding it. The greater the stillness, the greater its ability to pull you out of a state of frenzied activity into quiet. It represents hibernation, germination, and gestation and is especially helpful when giving birth to some new aspect of yourself.

Water colors

The colors associated with water in traditional feng shui are black and dark blue. Black represents the energy of still water. Dark like the womb environment, it is the energy of universal consciousness from which individual consciousness is born.

Adding black to your space encourages you to develop inner wisdom and strengthen your connection with divine forces through an in-depth study of the self. It is also associated with new beginnings. A lot of black will send a strong message that you are not interested in social interactions.

When you move from black to deep blues, you engage the energy of moving water. It is the energy of moving water that directly influences career and the flow of money into your life. If you desire more movement and social interaction in your career, use deep blues rather than black.

Water energy allows you to relax and release anything you might have picked up during the day. Starting or ending your day in a water room will help you feel clean and free, both physically and emotionally.

Water shapes & structures

Still-water shapes. Any structure that recreates the energy of the womb will strengthen still-water energy. The still-water shape is the lake or the pond, where energy slowly moves inward and becomes still. Although a pond is more of an object than a shape, any object that holds the shape of a pond, or pictures of a pond, will increase still-water energy.

Moving-water shapes. Any shape that induces flow carries the energy of moving water. Traditionally drawn as rippling waves, terraces, or cascades, moving-water shapes direct energy sideways or downward.

Moving water directs energy downward.

An attic room where the eaves come down around the person incorporates the still-water feature of a low roof. This space will feel more secure and protective than one with a vaulted ceiling.

To increase the energy of still water, add an aquarium without a pump or a vase with flowers.

Design ideas for increasing water

Still water. To increase the energy of still water, lower your lights and add soft cushions, a vase full of water, or an aquarium with a low pump. On the outside of your house, add a birdbath, pool, or a pond. In still water features, it is important to make certain that the water does not stagnate. Ponds should be cleaned regularly and indoor water should be changed daily.

The terraced steps leading down from the tub and the draped swag both increase the water element in this bathroom. The water is balanced by the strong wood energy in the tree outside the window and the upright wheat sheaves on both sides of the bath.

This outdoor pond incorporates water, wood (the greenery), and metal (the half-circle shape). Including at least three of the five elements in any feature promotes a balanced flow of chi.

Moving water. You can also increase downward movement by replacing horizontal blinds with drapes or by adding furniture pieces that slope, such as sleigh beds. Anything that hangs will increase water energy—mobiles, plants, jewelry, pots and pans, or even tools. Fish mobiles are a great traditional adjustment because both the fish and the downward movement of the mobile represent water.

Increase moving water with an indoor fountain as a symbol of abundance. If you place a frog next to the fountain, be certain he is leaping into the water, not away, or your abundance will also leave you.

Wood: personal growth

If you are interested in growth and creativity, think wood. Wood is the upward-moving energy that transforms seedlings into blooms and saplings into trees. Wood energy takes you beyond where you have been, and encourages you to be more, try more, and experience more. More focused than fire energy, wood energy is direct. It infuses your actions with purpose and meaning and promotes personal growth.

Wood energy is both the trunk of the tree, including the nurturing ability of the roots, and the branches that bend and move with the wind. It represents the union of earth (roots and trunk) and sky (branches and leaves) and the personal growth that comes from uniting those two forces.

Wood colors

Wood colors are clear and energizing, but not pastel. Traditional wood colors are green, which represents growth and healing, and purple, which represents abundance and expression. Avoid colors that have a lot of gray in them and appear muted or muddy; they slow growth.

Since the room has a low ceiling and ceiling beams, the vertical stripes painted on the wall lift the energy of the room. The tall wooden frames on the glass doors also generate the vertical flow of wood.

Wood shapes & structures

Wood shapes move energy in a vertical column, both securing roots and extending branches. Any shape or structure that shifts the flow of energy from horizontal to vertical strengthens wood.

Pillars. The triad of heaven, man, and earth is represented in the pillar. It is the force that connects the heavens with the earth, holding everything in between in a delicate balance. By incorporating pillars or columns in your home, you acknowledge your need for both heavenly guidance and earthly grounding. Pillars and columns should have rounded edges. If the edges are squared, you lose much of the vertical movement and create a problem with "poison arrows," the intense chi from a sharp edge.

Whether the pillar is simulated, as above, or is an actual pillar, at the right, this symbol unites earth energy with heaven energy for a peaceful balance.

Wood need not be heavy, such as this carved birdcage, which is especially auspicious since wood is related to the movement of air and wind.

Design ideas for increasing wood

Because wood energy connects us with the growth cycles of nature, any living plant will increase wood energy. Trees or plants that move upward, such as a ficus tree, are better choices than hanging plants. A hanging plant moves energy back down again.

When a rectangle is turned so the longest side is vertical, it generates a wood vibration. Therefore, to increase wood you would choose items that are opposite from an earth vibration. Instead of a side-by-side, you would choose a tall dresser. You would display a vertical painting rather than a landscape.

Tall windows and cupboards as well as ladder-back chairs or grandfather clocks will also add vertical rectangles increasing wood. Items that are made of wood, such as cooking utensils, cabinets, hutches, or railings, all increase wood energy.

The upward-moving plant in the corner, the pillars outside vertical windows, and the tall wooden bookshelves all increase the wood element in this room.

Walls. If you do not have pillars or columns in your home, you still have wood energy. Your walls are a connecting force between heaven and earth. They draw the energy of the earth up towards the sky and bring it back down again. They connect the roof with the foundation and stabilize the vertical movement of energy throughout the house. Increase wood energy in your home by emphasizing your walls. Wall treatments that include vertical patterns are powerful.

Vertical objects such as these bat rungs help move energy upward.

Using striped wallpaper or painting stripes generates wood energy. A faux painting of vines in this photograph directs the chi flow upward.

Working with the elements

Enhancing element energy

To enhance fire—add fire or wood elements (wood feeds fire and subdues earth). Design ideas: add tall chairs, pillars, palm trees or yucca trees, backlit plants, groupings of three, red or green candles, a carved wooden box, or lamps.

To enhance earth—add earth or fire elements (fire feeds earth and subdues metal). Design ideas: add terra-cotta pots, triple-wick yellow or red candles, large heavy items, brightly colored pillows, pottery, a rock garden, or warm cozy blankets.

To enhance metal—add metal or earth elements (earth feeds metal and subdues water). Design ideas: add low, wide furniture, a stone top on a metal table frame, long comfortable sofas, a brick pathway, metal chimes or bells.

To enhance water—add water or metal elements (metal feeds water and subdues wood). Design ideas: add rainbow windsocks, hanging plants, a copper fountain, a black or dark blue birdbath, a white vase, a curved path, or white tiles around the bath.

To enhance wood—add wood and water elements (water supports wood and subdues fire). Design ideas: add sloping or tall furniture pieces, a blue or green vase, flowing curtains, or vertical blinds.

Creating harmony & balance

Once you are familiar with the elements, there is a lot you can do to balance these elemental forces with colors, textures, composition, and shapes. This is not as daunting as it sounds, and incorporating it into your design will infuse your rooms with a sense of harmony and flow that is hard to pinpoint, yet is instantly noticeable.

Mapping elements

This exercise is helpful in getting a visual image of how balanced the elements are in your space.

1. Take a floor plan or draw a floor plan that shows walls, windows, and doors.

2. With colored pencils, color in a small area for each item that you can associate with a given element. For example, for the fireplace use red to mark a fire element, for the bathtub use dark blue to mark this water element.

3. Remember to mark items based on their shape or color as well as their composition. A black sofa is a water element, a brown chair is earth. A colorful floral arrangement that expands out at the top is a fire vibration and a pillar is wood.

4. For items that have more than a single element association, use some of each color when marking it. For example, if a pillar is white marble, it has an earth element (marble), a metal element (white), and wood (the pillar shape).

5. When you look at your element map, note the colors you have a lot of and the colors of which you have very little. The goal is balance. Usually a strong presence of at least three of the five elements will provide a balanced environment. Use decor to bring in missing elements or to subdue any dominating elements.

Using cycles of the elements

Because of the different ways in which energy from each of the five elements move, certain element combinations will support, or enhance, a certain energy flow. Others will reduce, or subdue, those same energies. These two element cycles are commonly referred to as the constructive (enhancing) and destructive (subduing) cycles.

The constructive cycle

In feng shui, you can strengthen the energy of an element in two ways: you can add more of the element, or you can add more of the enhancing element. The enhancing element gives its energy to the element you are trying to strengthen. For example, water feeds and generates growth in trees. Therefore, to strengthen wood energy in your home, you could add more water energy.

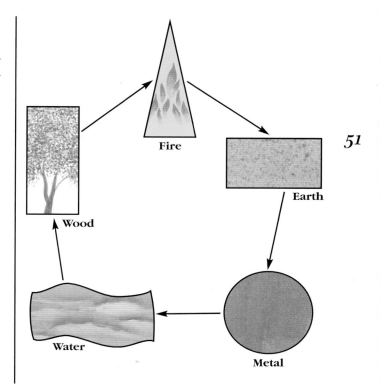

- ▲ Fire generates ash (earth)
- ▲ Earth forms ore (metal)
- ▲ Metal condensation produces water
- ▲ Water nourishes wood
- ▲ Wood feeds fire

The bright (fire) colors in the pictures, the upright (wood) chairs, the horizontal (earth) table, the blue (water) dishes, the white (metal) blinds, all work together to balance this room.

To subdue fire—add water or earth elements. Water subdues fire and earth drains it.

To subdue earth—add wood or metal elements. Wood subdues earth and metal drains it.

To subdue metal—add fire or water elements. Fire subdues metal and water drains it.

To subdue water—add earth or wood elements. Earth subdues water and wood drains it.

To subdue wood—add metal or fire elements. Metal subdues wood and fire drains it.

If you know Chinese astrology, you can compare your home composition to your astrological composition and see whether your home is strengthening or weakening your personal chi. For example, if you were born with no fire elements in your chart, and your home has very few fire elements in it, it will not balance out the lack of fire in your body.

Too much of a good thing becomes destructive. For example, water extinguishes fire, or earth is washed away by water taking out necessary energy to stay balanced. You can use the energetic properties of different elements to subdue energies that might be too strong and out of balance with the rest of your home.

Balancing elements in your personal chi

Use the following descriptions to determine whether you have a strong or weak presence of any given element in your physical body.

Fire energy in the body

↑ Too much fire energy can increase your feelings of anger and intense reactions. You might start to act rashly and not think things through adequately.

↓ Not enough fire can leave you feeling cold, distant, unattached from life and other people. You might even find you swallow your anger rather than express it.

✔ Just the right amount of fire energy will keep you feeling motivated, alive, full of vitality, and connected to others. You will laugh easily, and feel the kind of joy that courses through your body.

Earth energy in the body

↑ Too much earth energy causes smothering and stifling. You might feel stuck or worried that your loved ones will leave you. You can have a difficult time dealing with change and allowing abundance into your life.

↓ Not enough earth energy creates a strong concern with survival needs. You might not feel safe or secure and might tend to look to others to provide your safety and grounding. You might tend to leave your body and hang out in your head more often.

✔ Just the right amount of earth energy provides a sense of safety and security. You feel centered, grounded, and respect your physical body.

Metal energy in the body

⬆ Too much metal energy can make energy sharp—enhancing feelings of sarcasm, feeling nosy, self-righteous, or needing to belittle others. With too much charge in the air, it is hard to relax, contributing to increasing stress.

⬇ Not enough metal can make you feel scattered and confused. Because metal increases the ability to concentrate and focus, it can also heighten difficulty in verbal communication.

✔ Just the right amount of metal energy allows for clear, well thought-out communication among family members. No single person dominates conversations, each speaks in turn. You are able to assert yourself, without being abrasive or rude.

Water energy in the body

⬆ Too much water energy creates a tendency to be overly emotional. There might be frequent crying and distress with no way to get the emotional body in harmony with the mental, physical, and spiritual body. Too much still water can result in depression and stagnation. Too much moving water can result in the feeling that life is moving too quickly and you cannot keep up.

⬇ Not enough water leaves you feeling drained and emotionless. Things do not flow; finances are strained; people are not as helpful; everything requires an enormous amount of effort. You might feel that things are scarce and that there is never enough.

✔ Just the right amount of water energy helps you feel abundant, at ease, and in harmony with the world. You can feel and express your emotions without getting overly emotional. Finances stabilize and there is a feeling of security.

Wood energy in the body

⬆ Too much wood energy makes for stubborn people. Like the oak tree, you might grow rigid and lose the flexibility of the bamboo. You tend to become focused on your goals, issues, and concerns, ignoring others.

⬇ Not enough wood creates a situation where things change randomly, without control or reason. There is no rootedness; you might start a project and then change to a new project without finishing the first.

✔ Just the right amount of wood energy is the essence of human kindness. You listen with empathy and truly desire to support others. You think things through carefully, are a good listener, and find others' opinions interesting rather than threatening.

▲ Fire melts metal
▲ Earth muddies water
▲ Metal chops wood
▲ Water drowns fire
▲ Wood breaks up earth

If you find that you have too much or too little of a given element, you can use the constructive and subduing cycles to bring your body back into balance. Remember that whatever energies are present in your body will have an effect on your body. Use your home to balance, support, and enhance your natural tendencies.

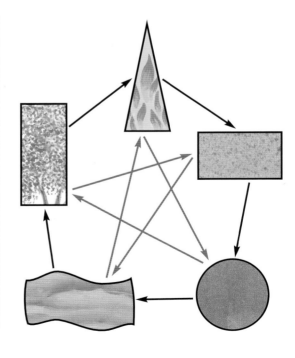

Places of safety

Feng shui priority number one is safety. You must feel safe and comfortable before you can risk expansion and growth. This means the most important overriding feng shui principle is creating safety in your home. You have probably read quite a few feng shui tips that related to safety, but never pulled all of them together into one category before. For example, Form School feng shui, the mother of all feng shui approaches, teaches that you should have the turtle at your back and the phoenix in front of you. In rather cryptic terms, what this is saying is to support your back (as a turtle in its shell) and provide open expansive energy in front (the phoenix represents transformation and expansion). Only when the back is supported can the front, the more public part of you, expand. To expose your back, such as placing your home on a cliff edge, weakens you. It drains chi and makes feeling safe difficult to achieve.

The turtle's shell has been a feng shui symbol of safety for many centuries.

This sandstone armchair is the perfect feng shui seat. With a high supportive back, low supportive sides, and an open expanse in front, this chair would make anyone sitting in it feel safe and in control.

The mirrored wall in this living room gives everyone a view of comings and goings. It equalizes what would otherwise be a striking inequality in the safety of various "sit" spots.

A commanding view

If you have ever been blindfolded and led around by the hand, you know just how scary it is to not know what is in front of you or coming up behind you. Being able to see who or what is coming is comforting because it gives you a moment to decide how you want to respond.

If you are sitting so that you cannot see the door, turn your seat around, if possible. It is best to place as much of your energy in front of you as possible. If your desk is attached to the wall, or some other feature prevents you from turning to face your door, place a convex mirror to open up your view while seated.

■ This chair is the least desirable place to sit, as the mirror exposes the back of this seat to everyone.

■ When your back is protected, as with the wall or screen, you feel safer.

■ The mirrored wall shown here allows anyone seated to see the door into the room, increasing a feeling of safety. If you are sitting so that you cannot see the door, turn your seat accordingly.

Solid wall behind you

No sitting area feels safe that has an exposed back. Just like the turtle in his shell, human beings feel better when have they some sort of protection behind them.

Although a solid wall is the best form of protection, a sofa table or plant behind a sitting area is better than nothing there at all.

Additionally, partial walls can be constructed through the creative use of screens, hanging fabric panels, or beaded curtains.

The right armchair (above) has an exposed back, which makes it feel unsafe. By turning the chair just a bit (below), it feels safer because the chair has more of its back against the wall.

Include retreat spaces

No one feels brave and courageous every day. If home holds places where you can retreat when feeling vulnerable or when you need a little time to regroup, it reduces your stress and anxiety levels. Set up to comfort the physical body and restore the spirit, retreat spaces have ways of filtering out the influence of the outside world. Such a filter could be a great sound system that floods the room with uplifting music. Another filter might be a protected view of passersby, so that you can watch but not be seen. One of my favorite filters is unplugging the phone and sitting down by the fire for an evening of board games with my two boys. If your home holds places where you can escape when things get to be too much, you will risk more, try harder, and push life to its envelope. When there is no place to retreat to, you will always hold part of yourself back.

This cozy window seat is tucked into a kitchen corner, making it possible to be close to other family members and still retreat. Any retreat space with a window is a great way to maintain connection with the outside world while rejuvenating your spirit.

Eliminate potential dangers

Remember the last time you had a horrible deadline hanging over you, invading your sleep and filling you with dread? Placing shelves with items on them directly above where someone will be sitting is the physical counterpart to that undesirable state. A common place to find such shelves is in the bathroom, directly above the toilet. To exacerbate the sense of impending doom, the shelf is usually shallow and the items hang over the edge. If you have existing shelves that you cannot move, fill them with lightweight objects such as baskets, towels, or a stack of pillows. Heavy or breakable items like books, pottery, vases, or glass knickknacks should be avoided.

This country room commits a number of feng shui sins. For starters, the propped picture above the fireplace has breakable items stacked in front of it. The potential that the picture could slip down, knocking all the breakables to the floor, creates constant unrest in the room. Other sins include breakable items on the floor, such as the vase, and a blocked fireplace.

Dirt is your friend. Just bringing in a potted plant will increase Earth energy in your home. Consider an indoor atrium, a miniature garden in a pot, or herbs growing in the kitchen. Plants link you to nature's cycles, as well as her grounding, reminding you that chi cycles through phases. Tuning in to nature's cycles can help bring your life into balance and bring your home into harmony with the environments with which it is meshed.

Potted plants are powerful yet simple ways to bring Earth inside to ground spirit.

He who plants a garden, plants happiness.
—Chinese proverb

Bring nature inside by using unadorned windows to open the garden view. Outdoor elements such as live plants and patio furniture can also be used indoors to increase Earth energy.

Connect to nature's grounding

Nothing helps you feel safer than connecting your own energy to something as large and stable and nurturing as Mother Earth. The physical earth can hold all of your stress and anxiety, and replace those feelings with a calm serenity that is hard to find elsewhere. When you learn to bring your body into connection with the earth's energy field, this is called grounding. You naturally feel steady, calm, and able to let go of any excess energy. The best way to ground your home is to bring Mother Earth inside. If you have ever spent time in a third-world country, walking on dirt floors and surrounded by straw walls, you have felt the powerful presence of Earth in the home. You can bring this presence into more-modern homes by contrasting polished surfaces with rough primitive textures, replacing plastics and synthetics with organic materials, and complementing overhead lighting with the warm glow of lit candles.

Containers

Containers are everywhere—in collections of antique glassware, coffee tins, carved wooden bowls, and woven baskets. Containers gather chi, helping you feel that there will be enough when you need it. They enclose and hold you and your things, uniting your need for psychological support with your material possessions. They represent Earth energy; and, just as soil that cannot hold rain cannot sustain life, a home without adequate containers cannot hold chi. In such a place, you will not feel supported or safe.

Full containers. If all your containers are full, your Earth energy tends toward the smothering and possessive side. Since full containers are a grounding energy, one that holds a pattern in place, too many full containers make it difficult to move your chi and do not allow for change. Disease and emotional difficulties can come as much from sluggish chi as from chi that moves too quickly. Break through excessive Earth with Wood energy. Place something green or tall in each container that must remain full, and remove as many unnecessary containers as possible. The traditional feng shui adjustment is to place bamboo (live or dried) in the container. Bamboo is considered the most aggressive wood element, breaking up even the hardest earth.

Empty containers. If you have a lot of empty containers, this is a strong indicator that you look to external sources for happiness and demand that others meet your needs because you feel unable to fill those needs yourself. Empty containers, in general, symbolize your inactivated potential. Although the pot has the ability to hold chi, it currently holds nothing. Sprinkling a few grains of rice in each container is a strong feng shui cure. The grains represent your ability to activate your potential and connect directly to the source (rice represents universal chi) rather than another person.

59

The ultimate in containerizing, this built-in Shaker wall unit is as beautiful as it is functional. You will want to put your things away if you create a beautiful and organized place to put them. A few hours spent with a professional organizer and a trip to the container store can change how you relate to "stuff" in general. Take the time to start enjoying all those things you worked so hard to acquire.

Make your containers suit your style. This ladder rack is more than a display item for vintage baskets, it provides useful storage and a playful approach to containerizing. If, like this owner, you do not want to fill all those baskets, be certain you put a couple of grains of rice in each one to keep the space energized.

Written intentions placed in a locked box or a letter hidden behind a mirror on the wall are ancient feng shui rituals for holding energy patterns in place.

If you have a home that holds no secret spaces, no hidden hole behind a sliding panel, no cubby underneath loose floorboards, make your own secret place. Hide it from company's eyes and limit access to it, as does this locked desk in the corner of a room.

We always fold ourselves away from others just enough to preserve a secret or two, something that we cannot share without destroying our inner landscape.
—Anne Roiphe

Secret spaces

We all have parts of us that have been lost, concealed from ourselves as well as from the outside world. Secret places are where we can rediscover that which has been lost. Once discovered, the hidden parts of ourselves can remain private until we feel ready and able to bring them out, piece by piece, into the world. In his book, *The Poetics of Space*, Gaston Bachelard expresses this fundamental human need:

"Wardrobes with their shelves, desks with their drawers, and chests with their false bottoms are veritable organs of the secret psychological life. Indeed, without these 'objects' and a few others in equally high favor, our intimate life would lack a model of intimacy. . . . It is not merely a matter of keeping a possession well guarded. The lock doesn't exist that could resist absolute violence, and all locks are an invitation to thieves. The lock is a psychological threshold. . . ."

You have a right to keep secrets. Secrecy provides the safety to be intimate and rigorously honest. Intimacy and honesty are absolutely necessary in getting to know and embrace yourself completely.

Closets can become intimate altars, secret spaces, and personal havens.

Closets as secret spaces.
I remember sitting in my mother's closet, trying on her shoes, coats, shawls, and hats. It was a way of "trying out" different possible futures, seeing myself as a grownup before I had to take on all the responsibilities of one.

Your closets behave as havens. They can keep things confidential and safe until you are ready to expose them. They can allow you a trial run with minimal risk. They can support your hidden desires through the pictures you paste up behind the wall of clothes hanging in your wardrobe.

Do not limit the function of your closets to storage. They can house intimate altars, function as meditation rooms, or become adventure caves for your children. Whatever you want to keep secret from the world, you can place in a closet. Closets will give you the time and space you need to figure out how to express that part of you in a graceful, balanced way.

Closets

Closets are a form of secret space. They have always been associated with the "shadow" aspects of the personality, a place to hide those things that the public persona does not wish to acknowledge or expose. "Coming out of the closet" and "skeletons in the closet" are two English phrases that reveal this association. More than just a place to hide or keep things secret, however, closets are also a place to put things on hold, allowing something to lie dormant and unexercised for a while. No one has the energy to deal with everything all at once. You need to be able to put some things aside to focus your energy. A home without closets feels unbearably exposed and overwhelming, and a psyche without enough quiet places to store things is equally so.

Full closets. You might think that full closets are the result of not having enough closets, but that is not the full feng shui meaning. Full closets indicate that the cycle of accumulation (a yin phase) is out of balance with the cycle of dispersion (a yang phase). Regardless of how many closets you have, the goal is balance. That means spending as much time and energy dispersing the items you no longer need as you do accumulating new items. Regardless of how much closet space you have, you need to let go of as many objects as are necessary to live in your current space with "comfort" and "ease." Comfort means having the ability to care for your present-time need—letting go of what you might need in the future, as well as what you picked up in the past. Ease means you are able to access what you need in your closets quickly and efficiently, without digging through piles or pulling out layers of stuff to reach something at the very back.

Simply by organizing what is in your closet, you can open up space.

I promise that the following process will bring order and success to your closet-clearing efforts:

- Think of your closets as a metaphor for your lungs. Chi needs to move in and out of the closet, just as air passes through your lungs. To get yourself ready to clear out your closet, open the door and leave it open for 24 hours prior to the clearing.

- Pull everything out and clean the floor. (All the heavy, lower-level vibrations sink to the floor over a period of time.)

- Sort your items into like piles, labeling each pile with a self-adhesive note as you create it.

- Place the least-used items back in the closet first, putting them toward the back and up high, where it is difficult to reach them.

- For closets that are stacked from top to bottom, use baskets or metal mesh containers to group the objects and to get them off the floor.

- For very full closets, consider painting the inside of the closet a bright yang color (a buttery yellow or a spring apple green) that will keep the chi moving even with all that stuff.

- Place the objects you use most in the front center portion of the closet, creating easy access.

- Step inside the closet and shut the door. If you have a hard time breathing, you need to let go of more.

- Continue releasing and reorganizing until you can go inside and breathe with ease—with the door shut.

Overexposing yourself

It is healthy to take risks, to open yourself to others, and to extend the hand of friendship. However, overexposing yourself is more an indication of a desperate need for connection and intimacy than an inclination to be neighborly. Common forms of overexposure include leaving the front door open all the time, not covering windows so that people can see in (especially at night), leaving windows open so that neighbors can overhear private conversations, and going outside in clothing (underwear, revealing pajamas) that is inappropriate for social situations.

If you find you tend to expose yourself too much, look for ways that you can share and connect with others that bring balance and self-respect. You will know you are not sharing yourself in a balanced way when others do not give of themselves to you the way you give to them. This is not a matter of you being more gracious or openhearted than they are; it usually means your need for connection overwhelms your interactions with others to the point where they begin to push you away.

Before placing the screen, this kitchen is exposed to everyone in the living room.

Placing the screen allows the owner control over how much of her kitchen is seen.

Feng shui adjustments, such as this screen, are as beautiful as they are practical.

Paper piles. Items on the ground can help ground you. However, if the environment is too heavy, or if you suffer depression or fatigue, you are experiencing too much of a good thing. One of the ways to lift the chi is to bring the items up off the floor just a few inches, so that energy can pass underneath. Place large heavy plants on plant stands that sit about three inches off the floor, stack items on shelves, replace the feet on couches or other furniture pieces, or even take a few items off the floor itself and place them on a table or shelf. Make these changes slowly, watching to be certain you are able to sustain your grounding without turning to other channels such as clutter, paper piles, or weight gain.

This entry hall benefited greatly from the addition of the few colorful pots of flowers, and a container for walking sticks. This is an example of how using objects on the floor to ground a room can be healthy. The white walls, hardwood floors, and intense color choices are strong yang components. They need something on the ground to pull the energy back down and help the space feel comfortable.

Items on the ground

Numerous items on the floor are often an attempt to "ground." Many factors in modern society will leave you seeking some grounding. Strong electromagnetic fields, virtual realities, an increasingly fast pace, and a lifestyle disconnected from nature's patterns and rhythms are only a few of these factors. As noted earlier in this chapter, grounding is the ability to forge a connection with the density and receptivity of Earth energy. An individual "grounds" in order to stabilize himself by connecting to the earth's enormous mass. Without enough grounding, you can feel scattered, distracted, full of inner turmoil, and confused.

If you find yourself placing numerous items low to the ground, ask yourself if you are trying to ground your energy. Items low to the ground will naturally bring your energy down lower in the body. When your energy settles into your *dan tien,* the body's natural energy center about four inches below the navel, you feel more grounded and connected to the natural world.

Furniture

The size, shape, and design of your furniture affects how comfortable you feel sharing your ideas and creations with others. To feel safe enough to share, your furniture needs to both support and express you.

A simple item with an unusual shape can express volumes.

Balanced furniture does not mean every piece must be the same size. Here, the large upholstered chair and substantial spool table are balanced by the shallow narrow book cabinet along the wall and the small chair that serves as a table or a footstool.

As tempting as it was to squeeze this tall armoire into the room, it actually constricts the chi flow because it does not leave enough space on top.

Streamlining your storage with built-ins eliminates the chi constriction and allows for more flow.

Larger-than-life furniture. When furniture is larger than the body that fills it, it feels much like a knight's armor, shielding you from the energy and opinions of others who might enter your space. Sometimes oversized furniture is necessary to fill an oversized room (See **When your gathering place is too large** on page 112), but it will make interactions more formal and limit how much people relax while in your home.

Find out what specific meaning your large furniture has for you by answering the question, "What kind of a person has large furniture?" Some responses I have heard to this question are:

- rich people,
- stately people,
- important people,
- fearful people,
- impostors,
- cold people.

Feng shui suggests that the size of a desk or a chair sends a strong message about how important you think you are. The ideal chair is one that supports your entire frame, comes high up the back, and provides armrests. If it is too large, however, it will dwarf you and make you look small and helpless inside it. The same goes for your desk, dining table, or living-room sofa. If you find that your furniture is too large, the following things can help you soften its effects in your space.

- Add lamplight and dimmers to blur the harsh edges and straight lines of large furniture with soft light.
- Include a dynamic, organic focal point. A fish tank with lively colorful fish, an indoor atrium, or even a decorative bowl of wheat grass can draw the eye away from the furniture and make the space feel more lively.
- Drape slipcovers over dining chairs.
- Bring in smaller decor pieces that are playful in nature, such as a hand-painted lamp, a collage, or a humorous sculpture.

Walls

The purpose of a wall is to serve as a barrier from external forces and to provide support for the entire structure—the thick adobe of the Southwest, the primitive concrete of a city loft, the whitewashed timbers of a California beach house.

Thick walls. Usually made from mud, brick, or plaster, thick walls are a wonderful way to provide supportive Earth energy. Thick Earth walls also allow for texture and aging, which connotes that support is long lasting, not temporary. If your walls are paper thin, they cannot physically support the weight of the house (See **Cracked walls** below) and do not help you feel safe or protected. Visually increase the thickness of your walls by texturizing existing walls (this works over lathe and plaster and over Sheetrock®), adding a stucco finish, using a layered-paint technique, or wallpapering. These thickening techniques will also "age" your walls, increasing timeless feel.

Cracked walls. Cracked walls represent a damaged support system and need to be mended as soon as possible. Simply covering up or hiding cracked walls is not sufficient. Covering cracks simply means that you are ignoring the fact that you do not feel supported. If you continue to exert your energy to reach your objectives, without taking the time to reestablish your connections with external sources of support, you will wipe yourself out. When repairing cracked walls, put forth your best effort to repair strained or damaged relationships, reconnect with nature, or tune in to your inner connection to "Source."

Thick walls represent a strong support system and help people feel safe and supported by their environment.

Adding a textured finish thickens walls and increases the safety factor of the home.

Why not go out on a limb?
That is where the fruit is.
—Will Rogers

This lovely collection of South American art and colorful tapestries punctuate this sitting area with personality and style. It is the personal, the unexpected, and the bold that give a room its zip.

The inspiring home

Stretch, grow, risk, challenge, deepen, expand, refine. Anchored in a safe, steady home, you are able to open and look at parts of yourself that would otherwise remain behind locked doors. However, a safe haven is only healing if you leave it once in a while. Safe colors, textures, and arrangements are meant to be the fodder for growth, not the ends in themselves. This is why a house with nothing but square shapes and brown earthy colors feels like it is missing something. Like the soil, the safe home without elements of surprise, growth, and change feels barren.

Let yourself soar

Safety features anchor chi in the home, moving it low to the ground and slowing the flow. Chi that has slowed to a standstill brings stagnation, fatigue, and disease. Homes must also contain features of expansion to balance this slowing. The symbol for expansion in Form School feng shui is the phoenix. Just as the turtle protects its back, the phoenix rises up from the ashes, having transformed challenge and risk into soaring, unrestrained energy. The rising phoenix is not meant to stay chained to the earth; it heads for the open sky. Give your interior world sky, as well as earth, and your wings will unfold.

How does the philosophical concept of "sky" translate into interior design? All features that open your energy body, activate a stronger chi flow, and speed up the rate at which your chi is moving are expansion features. Chi needs to move up and out, pushing through any boundaries or blocks, to send your spirit soaring. A spot of blue in an otherwise brown vase, a silk scarf in a pile of linens, or a star-shaped pillow against a rectangular sofa, all surprise the eye and wake the sleepy chi.

Disguise blank walls.
Protective supporting walls are great, but not when they block your ability to expand. For example, walking through your front door to be greeted by a blank wall just a few feet in front of you is considered bad feng shui. Why? Because it cripples your ability to expand your chi immediately upon entering your home. The phoenix does not have enough time to get off the ground before its flight is stopped. If the eye can perceive something in the distance, the energy to move forward is mobilized. With no views into interior rooms, no enticing curve of color or form, those energy reserves are never activated.

A collection of miniature African masks brings interest to a previously blank wall.

Unexpected views; personalized collections; and unique combinations of colors, shapes, and structural elements are the interior alchemist's formula for a blue sky. Here a window frame in a garden bed adds a startling visual accent to excite the chi.

Signs of growth

Plants that have outgrown their pots are not encouraged by the surrounding soil to continue growing. Likewise, home owners that have filled every last surface or bit of closet space are bound to feel stuck and stymied if they try to move forward. Of course, it is easier to repot your plants than it is to buy a new home every time you outgrow your existing one. Still, you have only three options. You can increase the size of your home by adding new rooms or closets, you can decrease the amount of things in the home, or you can organize those things in such a way as to open up more space between items. You need to decide which of these three options, or which combination of the three, is viable for you.

An otherwise wasted wall area flanking a window became home to a pair of matching bookshelves with storage underneath, increasing the functionality as well as the beauty of the space.

Selecting gatekeepers

Clutter clearing is a hot feng shui topic; however, it is important to distinguish between "clutter clearing" and letting things go. For someone who stores precious objects or family heirlooms for future generations to think of these objects as clutter is next to impossible. These items are not junk, rather they are collected life experiences stored in material form. What, to an outsider, might look like a lot of knickknacks are life vignettes built over generations of use. For many, releasing the experiences from the forms is incredibly difficult—the two seem inseparable.

I use a process of transferral to help clients through this difficult stage. I ask them to select those objects that have the most luminosity surrounding them, that function as gatekeepers to entire chunks of family history. A client might be storing three different sets of china, for example, or many boxes of old clothes. Selecting these objects can be a time-consuming process and it is important to support the person during this time. Once a client selects these objects, the energy of other like objects can be transferred to the holding objects.

The transfer happens by placing a holding object next to a similar object and visualizing the light in the similar one moving over and increasing the luminosity of the holding object. Sometimes it helps clients to hold both items, so that they can feel this energy transfer take place. Once the life force of an object is transferred to the holding object, letting that item pass to another home is much easier.

Rearranging what is there. When common objects are grouped together, they require less space and less energy. A closet jam-packed with old clothes, sheets, journals, towels, and piles of board games can transform into an organized and functioning space by taking the time to sort, fold, tidy, and stack these items neatly.

The most wonderful part about getting organized is that when you place like items with like, they energetically meld into one item. Instead of carrying the emotional and energetic weight of dozens of separate items in any given closet, you meld these items into groupings of three or four. The time and energy it takes for you to manage these items in the future is greatly reduced.

71

Items such as these Buddhas can function as gatekeepers, holding and storing the energy of an entire chunk of family history.

The risers and railings in a staircase lift eye, chi energy, and spirit.

Vertical lift

As your eye ascends, so does your chi. Pillars, columns, crown molding, and vertical structural features send chi energy spiraling upward. An interesting piece of wood at the top of a doorway, or the transfer of an outdoor porch pillar to your living room are unique expressions of vertical energy that can inspire your imagination as well as lift your chi. Imagination is the parent of creative expression, and light, high vibrations are most conducive to this mental art form. Look down at your feet and see how difficult it is to think creatively while gazing directly downward.

The carved wooden lintel brings the eye up above the doorway, raising the chi in the room.

Add a color splash

A startling burst of color can be just the thing to liven a drab room. Consider seasonal flowers, a throw, or candles as simple methods of including intense color without the overwhelm.

Find your edge

Although I am not an advocate of perching items precariously on shelves or other like surfaces, sometimes moving an item just an inch or two toward the edge of a table or mantel can completely change how "daring" the room feels.

A splash of color can increase your willingness to take risks.

This little horse perched just close enough to the edge of the mantel, makes things interesting. Sometimes a single item is all that is needed to bring a sense of adventure into a room.

A few things I always ask my students about their pictures are:

- If you drew just the face of your house, do you rely on external sources to help you define who you are?

- If you drew people, do you see your home as relating to the people who live there?

- If you drew trees, plants, or other natural elements, do you feel connected to the natural world and able to draw comfort and strength from it?

- Is there any part of your house that exists, which you have failed to draw?

- If so, do you energetically cut yourself off from that part of the house?

- Is the house in your drawing accessible, or hidden and isolated?

The right amount of exposure

As comfortable as it is to sit safely ensconced in your home, you need to venture out and connect with the outside world. One of my favorite workshop exercises is to have participants draw their homes on pieces of paper without giving them any guidelines or indications of what I will be looking for when they are done. (If you want to try this yourself, stop reading now and draw your house. Then continue reading to see what your drawing reveals about how you connect to the world.) Some draw their floor plan, others draw just the fronts of their houses, and others draw the inside, the outside, the city lights, the neighboring trees, the park around the corner, and the grocery store down the street.

What a person draws is a powerful indicator of how connected they feel to the world around them. If someone includes their pet cat but not their husband in their drawing, it may have interesting psychological implications. For those who link their house to the city by drawing streets but do not add a single tree, the implications are different, but nonetheless, richly revealing.

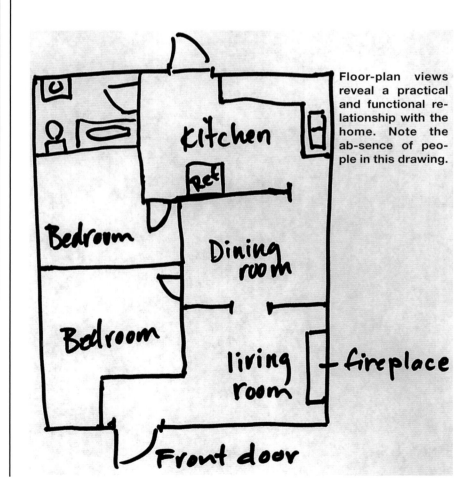

Floor-plan views reveal a practical and functional relationship with the home. Note the ab-sence of people in this drawing.

The originator of this drawing has connected her house to the natural world by including a tree, sun, grass, and surrounding shrubs.

This drawing indicates that the owner feels connected to the other people in the neighborhood. Roads (a means of access) have also been included.

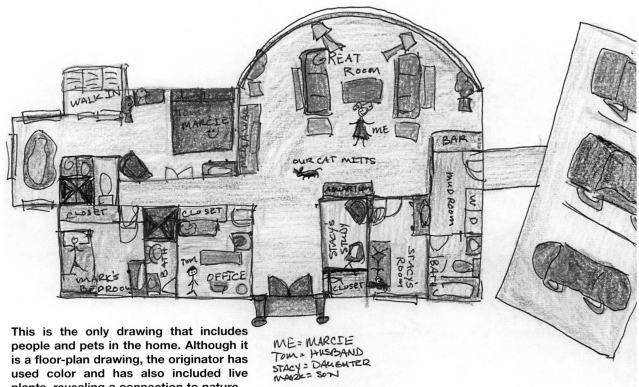

This is the only drawing that includes people and pets in the home. Although it is a floor-plan drawing, the originator has used color and has also included live plants, revealing a connection to nature.

Empty closets

In the last chapter, we talked about closets as secret spaces that empower you to try new things. Empty closets (and empty rooms) are a bit different. An empty closet indicates that the anabolic (breaking down) processes in a person's life are stronger than the catabolic (building up) processes. In the terms of Chinese medicine, the yang overwhelms the yin, creating an inability to hold onto much of anything for long, including friends, jobs, and hobbies. Empty closets also tend to reflect a life that is still on hold, waiting to be activated. Until there is purpose, there is no need to draw to you the things you need to fulfill that purpose.

To fill the empty closet, you need to connect to your life's purpose. In feng shui, purpose relates to *li*. Li is the natural, organic purpose as evident in form. As with the veins in a leaf or the markings on jade, each organism has a natural pattern or expression that arises from within. Discovering and expressing your li is how you find your way in the natural flow and order of life. To find your li, place an item in the closet that displays its pattern, such as a shell or a rock. Leave the item in the closet for as long as it takes to attract to you the things you need to fulfill your purpose. Let it serve as a magnet, drawing the people, situations, opportunities, and resources you need to discover and give your gifts in the world.

If you are struggling to find a deeper sense of purpose, place a leaf in your empty closet. The leaf contains everything it needs within itself, its pattern artfully displayed as tiny veins across a papery membrane.

As with the veins in a leaf or the markings on jade, each organism has a natural pattern or expression that arises from within.

This woven box can be used to catch, hold, and transform negative thoughts, fears, or emotions. As you interact with an empty room, identify and write down any fears or difficult emotions that come up for you and stuff them in your basket or container. The container will do the work of transforming them.

Rooms cut off from the rest of the house

Whether access to a room is physically limited or it just feels that way, some rooms are separate from the chi flow of the house. These rooms are dormant, rarely entered, and have a lower chi force. In some cases, usually when someone has lost their partner and is living alone in the house, an entire side of the house feels separate and lifeless.

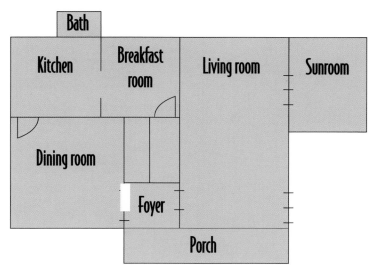

This house plan demanded that a door be opened from the foyer to the dining room, thus connecting it to the rest of the house. Before reconstruction, one had to walk from the foyer through the living room, the hallway, the breakfast room, and the kitchen to reach the dining room.

Ba gua map

Abundance	Fame/ reputation	Intimate relations
Family/ ancestors	Health	Children/ creativity
Self knowledge	Journey/ career	Helpful people

Entrance

Merging the room with the house. When one room is removed from the chi flow of the house, first figure out which ba gua sector the room is in. (See the Ba gua map below, or turn to page 146, for more information on ba gua mapping.) Ask yourself how you are currently feeling about that area of your life. In what ways might you feel cut off or estranged? For example, if the room falls into Family and Ancestors, do you feel isolated or removed from your family circle in some way? Did you choose to leave for some reason? If the room falls into Helpful People, do you desire to be an accepted integral part of a thriving community, yet find yourself playing the role of the loner or outsider? If the room is in Self-knowledge, are you a stranger to your own inner needs and desires, afraid of spending time alone?

When you discover what part of your inner terrain is represented by your vacant or separate room, you will know whether you are ready and willing to reconnect with that part of you. If you are willing, you can begin the merger.

You will need one of three objects: a woven basket with a lid, a hollowed-out gourd, or a piece of pottery with a narrow neck at the top. These containers are traditionally used to catch, hold, and transform any negative thoughts, fears, or emotions. Place this object in the room. Next, unblock any doors or windows that do not open. If there is a door you can open but always leave shut, open the door. Draw back shades and blinds to allow as much "light of day" into the room as possible. Place something in the room that you will need to care for, such as a few plants, a fountain, or a pet bird.

Sitting areas with access to natural light draw comfort.

Turn your face to the sunshine and all shadows fall behind.
—Helen Keller

The force of light

More than any other force, light represents nature's ability to bring life force into the home. A home that does not receive enough natural light gradually loses its life force and becomes unable to activate or energize the people living there. (See **Illumination** on pages 297–298 for information on how seasonal lighting affects the body.)

Natural light infuses this room with a vibrant intensity that lifts the spirit and energizes the body.

Light on two sides. Years ago, the authors of *A Pattern Language,* Alexander/ Jacobson/Silverstein, made the claim that every room needs natural light on two sides in order to feel balanced. Without light on at least two sides of a room, the lit wall would be too bright, and the remaining space would fall into shadow. I have tested their statement for the past eight years and must agree that every room feels better if it has at least two walls that allow natural light into the room. This light does not need to come directly from a window, however. It is possible to get your light through a doorway into an adjacent room or by replacing part of an interior wall with glass blocks, an interior window, or a mirror.

A light in the tunnel. Some rooms are positioned directly in the center of the house and have no access to natural light at all. Solar tubes are a great modern invention that can solve this problem some of the time. Installed on the roof, a solar tube can bring light down a tube into rooms that have no exterior walls, such as an interior bathroom. However, if you have living space above you, you cannot use this method. Compensate for a lack of light by adding a fan and live green plants to the room. Clear out heavy items if you can and paint the walls a light color. These adjustments will increase the yang energy in the space and help balance the lack of light.

Adding windows on the right created a balanced flow of light and chi, making this room a delightful place to be. A similar effect could be achieved with a mirror.

This chair is too large for the room and creates a chi block.

Selecting a smaller chair for beside the fireplace brought the room back into balance.

Furniture

In the previous chapter, we addressed the issue of furniture that was too large. But furniture is much more than a place to sit. Your tables, chairs, lamps, and sofas are powerful vehicles for self-expression. A blue buffet in the dining room, a whimsical lamp shade, or an antique mail cupboard becomes a vessel by which the soul travels through the physical realm. These items are much more than decorative. Their painted surfaces reflect your smiles and the contents of their drawers reveal your dreams.

Diminutive furniture. When your furniture is too small, it is challenging to assert yourself. Your home base is communicating to you that you are small and insignificant. When guests come and sit in chairs that are too small to hold them, they will wonder if you are capable of taking care of yourself. Although smaller furniture is sometimes necessary in small spaces, make certain that you supplement small furniture pieces with an underlying message of strength and self-reliance.

- Add bold wall color or intense spots of color in your decor items.
- Use materials that last a long time, such as a leather couch or a hardwood desk.
- "Self-soothe" and care for your needs with candles, a stereo, and a comfy footstool.
- Add living plants to expand the chi and help your guests feel expansive, even if the chair they are sitting in is small.
- Place your wall art a few inches lower than normal to decrease the scale of the room and help the furniture feel larger.
- Add enough furniture so that the space does not have gaping holes where the chi flow stalls.

Simply opening a window can jump-start your chi and increase the energy in a room.

Too much furniture. The accumulation of stuff is the same for furniture as it is for other items. Too much slows the chi flow and prohibits movement, change, and the ability to take action. The more yin a person is, the greater the tendency to fill up every last inch of space. Start by getting the chi moving before you even move any furniture.

- Hang a large 1½ inch or 2 inch (40 mm or 50 mm), round, faceted crystal in the center of the room or home. The crystal will send chi out 360 degrees, breaking up old and rigid patterns, making it easier for you to begin a new pattern.
- Open your windows and drapes more, letting in both light and fresh air.
- Turn your lights on more often, even during the day.

The furniture density in this room inhibits chi flow. To get the chi flowing here again, remove the trunks and replace them with a small side table. Straightening the ottoman and shifting the dining area a foot to the right would also improve the area.

When you are ready to remove furniture:

- Start by removing small pieces, such as an occasional table or an extra lamp.
- Remove pieces that block you from accessing other parts of the house—a chair that blocks a door, a dresser that keeps you from opening a window.
- Work slowly, one or two items at a time, allowing your body time to adjust to each change before you remove additional items.
- Find great new homes for the items you remove to create a win/win situation for all.
- Consider moving some favorite items to a porch, patio, or garden setting.

82

A wall of windows becomes its own canvas, allowing the owners of this room to view a constantly evolving display of color.

Walls

What is on the walls? Walls are the canvas, you are the artist. What you place on your walls is as creative and as telling as the strokes on the canvas. Wall art sends a strong message as to what you value: your relationship with your own creative ability; your financial situation; your relationship with your family-of-origin, your children or spouse; and your overall disposition and approach to life.

So what does it mean if you have nothing at all on your walls? In general, barren walls mean a lower level of chi. Whether they are barren because you think you cannot afford to buy anything (relationship to money), cannot decide what to hang (blocked creativity), or are waiting for something else to happen first (passivity), the result is the same. Your chi remains in an inactive state of potential and needs to be activated.

Selecting wall art. Choosing something for your walls is like building your CD collection or selecting books for your library; you are essentially designing your life by what you choose. Because what you place on your walls cannot help but reveal your inner values, strengths, and relationships, it provides a tremendous opportunity for manifestation, but can also create much fear of failure. This fear can keep people stuck with bare walls for years.

Most people know what they do not want before they can identify what they do want. Select a wall where you know you want to put something, and place whatever you can lay your hands on there. Pick something up at a garage sale or hang a sheet if you have nothing. The point is that, after you hang something there, your mind will begin to tell you what it is that you do want. You will hear something along these lines. "That is way too small, the piece is going to need to be at least 24 inches by 36 inches." Or, "I want brighter colors here." Or, "It needs to be subtle and something old to calm the room. I don't want to make a loud garish statement." Besides stimulating your mind, hanging something will also jump-start your chi. You will feel activated by the placement just because you got your energy moving again. Sometimes you need this type of chi boost before you have the resources necessary to make the difficult choices or paint the wall.

This painting of a receding staircase transports the viewer to a magical realm.

Children often make the best artists. This owner enlivened her corner with a totem pole of decorated ceramic cups made by her child's art class.

Setting up a living space

If you have read a few feng shui books, you probably have quite a long list of what you should do in your space, but feel a bit overwhelmed as to how to make it all happen. Relax. No one can follow every feng shui rule in every room, and to try to do so usually leaves you with a room that feels contrived and ill-suited to your actual needs. This chapter will take you through the process of setting up a living room using feng shui principles, and help you to understand the sequencing behind the finished result.

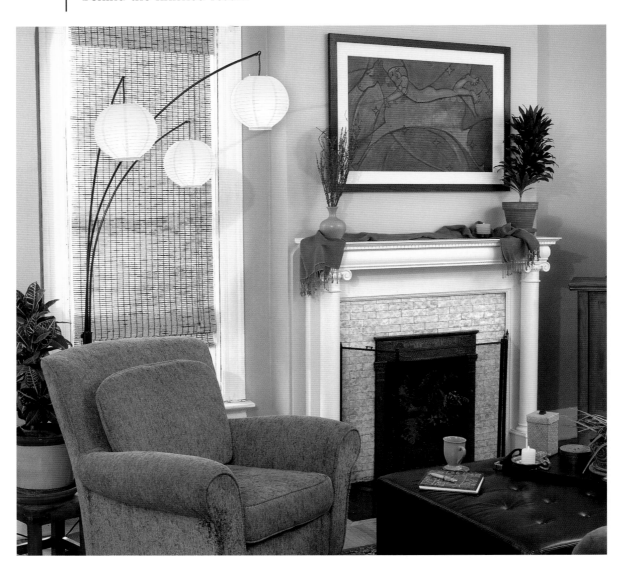

Before feng shui

Originally, my client had placed the couch in front of the window in order to reserve the solid wall for the TV. Unfortunately, this placed the TV directly opposite the fireplace. This placement created a strong line of chi energy between the fireplace and the TV and divided the room in half. The couch in front of the windows also weakened the chi of the window, which was the most beautiful feature of the room, and weakened the chi of anyone sitting on the couch, since cold air seeped through in the evenings.

Stage one—begin with an empty room

To begin, you must empty the room of furniture in order to feel what is happening before you add any of your "stuff." Decide first how you will use the room; then, place the furniture. In this case, the dark brown wall color made the room feel like a tomb and the lack of light left the owner feeling depressed and sluggish in the winter. Although the owner wanted to lighten things up, she was worried about losing her grounding, since she tended to move very quickly through life, taking on one project after another and never completing them. She liked the size of the room, and did not want it to feel too formal.

The original couch placement blocked the windows, diminishing their beauty and ability to energize the room.

Based on the previous information, my client and I made the following decisions:

85

- We selected a light wall color that was also warm and earthy. This way the light could bounce and move through the room, but the owner still felt safe, stable, and grounded in the space. We created a custom gold with hints of green that has enough pigment to hold chi in the space, yet is light enough to allow easy movement and chi flow.

- We chose window treatments that allowed the light in. The light must penetrate as far into the room as possible, so we needed something that could be up and completely out of the way during the day. We selected natural bamboo Roman shades that allow light in and give a view of the nearby park. The bamboo keeps the room feeling earthy and in touch with natural forces.

- We removed anything artificial. The plastic ceiling medallions felt both artificial and too formal. The owner likes the light fixtures, so she simply removed the medallions above them.

Stage two—enter the primary players

With the room painted and ready to go, it was time to place the largest, most troublesome pieces in the room to get a sense of how large they were and possible placements.

We started with the rug, the TV, the couch, and a reading chair. I asked the owner how she intended to use this furniture. Who would sit where and what functions must each piece support? She wanted the rug/floor space to stay open so that she could perform her Pilates™ workout here without having to move things. The couch will serve many functions, including reading with her son in the evening, casual entertaining, chats with friends, snuggling with her husband while watching the news at night, and glancing at people out the window during the day. The chair will be used for reading and as a place for her to come and sit by herself. She uses this area both first thing in the morning and late at night.

■ With the rug laid out, the couch was the first placement. Since no one always gets to have everything necessary for perfect feng shui in their home, we worked out a solution that at first "seemed" contradictory, yet in reality works quite well.

■ We placed the couch on the solid wall facing the fireplace, restoring the fireplace as the room's designated focal point.

The decision to place the couch against the solid wall restored the room's focal point and provided a solid wall behind sitting areas.

Once these placements were made, it was easy to place the additional objects. The two large plants were positioned in front of the windows both to hold the chi in the room and to frame the center window. This left the intake vent open and allowed for better air circulation. The owner's prize original artwork was hung over the fireplace, since this area was now the uncontested focal point. Other plants and small tables filled in the corners and provided spots to set down drinks and books.

- The TV was next. Since the rest of the room was all windows or open to the adjacent dining room, we angled the TV in the corner of the room, subduing its presence while giving the owner a prime viewing alignment from the newly positioned couch. Although the TV covered part of the side window, the placement allowed chi to flow behind it so that it did not cut the windows off from the rest of the room the way the couch had.

- The chair needed to be segregated. However, it had to be close enough that someone sitting in it could also see the TV and join
in the conversation when desired. We angled it on the other side of the fireplace, complementing the angle of the TV and drawing the energy of the room toward the center.

With the couch gone from the window, we needed the plants to keep the chi force inside the room. Otherwise, the pull from the park across the street was too great.

Stage three—supply what is missing

When you move from house to house, you rarely have just what you need in order to make things work in the new space. Oftentimes rooms are larger than in the previous house (as with families who are moving from starter homes to larger family homes). However, sometimes they are smaller (as with reduced family size or other events requiring downsizing).

In this particular home, the new living room was larger than the previous one. The rug felt too small for the new space and people sitting on the couch seemed to yell across the room to the person sitting in the chair. The two sides of the room were still not connecting, resulting in stilted conversation. The space lacked the cozy feel of their previous smaller living room. It needed something, but what?

Adding plants in front of this window and at each corner of the room anchored a similar room and prevented the chi from escaping out the front window.

Without something in the center, the sides of this room pull apart, the chair and couch are too far away from each other, and conversation will be more difficult.

- The square ottoman could be used by both the person sitting in the chair and anyone sitting on the couch, whereas a typical coffee table or a rectangular ottoman could be reached only by someone on the couch. People now tend to lean in toward the center of the room and connect with each other, since the ottoman/table is the new place for drinks, magazines, etc.
- The ottoman/table is quite lightweight and easy to move, which makes it possible for the owner to slide it over and continue her Pilates in the room.
- The dark brown color grounds the center of the room (balancing out the large front windows), contains the chi flow, and revitalizes the space.
- The square shape, besides being another grounding influence, makes it easy to walk around all four sides of the piece without feeling blocked or constricted.

89

When moving from a smaller space to a larger one, add plants. Their life force will fill the larger room and eliminate the need to purchase additional furniture.

Adding the ottoman brought both sides of the room together and increased the social nature of the room. With coasters and a serving tray to protect its surface, it acts as a coffee table.

■ The only lamps in the room were across the room from the reading area, making it awkward to use lamplighting without overhead lighting. The living room and dining room were energetically lopsided, because the pull of the park view was considerably stronger than any view in the dining room.

■ The final addition was actually placed in the dining-room area that opened into the living room. A large horizontal mirror was hung on the dining-room wall facing the park. The mirror brought all the colors and beauty of the park into the dining room, and also activated the entire space between the front living-room window and the rear dining-room wall. This brought the two rooms back into balance and left everyone who entered feeling vitalized and energetic.

Each room has its own trouble spots. Maybe your troubles include floor radiators or a room with too many doors. Whatever is making it difficult for you, remember to position things according to how you and your family want to use the space, rather than by rules in a book. You will notice all these changes were made to balance out and support the needs, tastes, and tendencies of the family members who live in the space. Feng shui is not a list of dos and don'ts to be strictly applied. It is a process of understanding how the structures and patterns of a physical space impact the people who live and work there. Once you see how your home is influencing your interactions, you can shift your home to support your life.

In this case, we did not solve the problem by focusing on just the living room. We had to look to an adjoining room for the answer.

The mirror above the sideboard reflects the adjoining room and connects both rooms visually.

Room for one

The bathtub is an ideal place to spend time alone. Taking just a moment to light a few candles, add essential oils, and include bath salts can make this time sacred.

All man's miseries derive from not being able to sit quietly in a room alone.

—Pascal

Time alone—it petrifies some of us and comforts others. Regardless of how you feel about spending time alone, you will probably acknowledge that no one can be comfortable in the presence of others until one can be comfortable alone. Said a different way, others will be more comfortable in your presence when you spend time with you.

Creating comfort in alone spaces

"Make yourself at home" is a phrase we commonly use when guests come to visit. However, what does it mean to make yourself at home? What does it mean to be "at home" at all? For me, being at home is being comfortable in my own skin. Universally, it means knowing ourselves, liking ourselves, and accepting all of who we are. Alone spaces are vital in this process of knowing, liking, and accepting the self. A room for one opens the necessary space for internal reflection, exploration, and play. When you have your own space, you can feel what it is to "be you." Without this space, many of us are left wondering just who we are.

Encouraging time alone

Depending on your five-element composition, you may have a problem spending time alone. People with either high-Wood or high-Fire energy have difficulty sitting still and being by themselves. Your reason for avoiding alone time should govern the creation of your private space.

Adding bamboo to any room is a simple way to make Wood energy feel at home.

Still unable to settle your Wood? Give yourself a green chair to sit in. Since Wood energy is drawn to green, you will be more likely to sit down. Prop your feet up on a footstool and wrap your legs in a blanket to give yourself that bit of extra enticement to stay seated.

Overcoming Wood's tendencies. If you have a lot of Wood energy, you need to be doing something all the time—even when you are alone. No problem. Set up alone spaces that allow for solitary activities such as fly tying, knitting, or charting your next vacation. The shower or bath is also a great place for you to be alone. The downward moving Water energy helps drain your excessive Wood and allows your busy mind and body to relax. Consider making evening baths your daily meditation.

Finding Fire's way. Fire energy is not at all interested in a day of solitude. In fact, being alone is Fire's greatest fear. Fire wants to merge and expand and, most of all, share. The best way for Fire to become comfortable with being alone is to view this as a preparation time for future sharing. If you have a lot of Fire, spend your first few "alone" hours in creative expression of your gifts and dreams. Make a collage or try painting a watercolor. Over time, you will begin to find that you have more to share with others socially because you have spent time with yourself.

This space might be overwhelming for some, but Fire energy finds itself through artistic expression, rather than through internal reflection. Colorful fabrics might be the only way to get Fire to take a seat.

Incorporating altars

An altar is a means of focusing your energy on particular connections. Spiritual altars focus this energy on your relationship with the divine; however, altars need not necessarily be about a connection with the divine, but they are meant to lift spirit.

The spiritual altar. The most common form of altar is a spiritual altar. This type of altar holds objects that help the individual feel personally connected to the divine. Although religious icons are common for this type of altar, any object that represents a personal connection will strengthen the energy of that connection. Think beyond the canned associations of your religious upbringing. What places in nature have inspired the "awe" of the divine in you? What objects inspire moments of personal reflection and internal exploration? What items remind you of your life's purpose and your connection to spirit through that sense of purpose? Use these items to build a personal altar that stirs your soul and comforts your heart every time you look at it.

The community altar. This type of altar was created by a group of feng shui practitioners who come together once a year to share in the energy of community. The altar was assembled by each person bringing an object that represented universal life force to them. After the energies of these objects had been joined through ritual, the individuals who took them home at the end of the retreat brought the energy of the entire group home, as well as their object. You can use community altars to draw the supportive loving chi of a group of friends into your home.

94

You can make an altar anywhere. This goddess figure and a small candle can transform a kitchen counter into sacred space.

A bathroom shelf dedicated to communion with the divine can "altar" the energy field of the entire house.

Traditionally, altars were made from religious icons. This Virgin Mary blesses all who enter here.

The travel altar. In traditional Tibetan culture, people took personal altars with them when they traveled. These altars were usually an icon wrapped with incense in a cloth. Consider making a travel altar that will allow you to bring the energy of home with you whenever you spend time away. Items that hold energy, such as rocks, strips of cloth, or incense sticks, make good travel altars.

The nature altar. This form of altar is sometimes called a nature sanctuary. It is a place on your land that you set aside for the nature spirits and devas. By definition, this altar is not man-made. Rather than "creating" a nature altar, ask the nature spirits what place in your yard they would like to have as their own. Keep this area untouched, allowing things to grow wild. You might even want to put up a decorative border to let others know that this special place is off limits and should not be touched by humans. You will find that devoting a portion of your space to nature opens a respectful partnership between yourself and natural forces that will benefit your life in many ways.

Untouched land becomes a nature sanctuary and a tribute to nature's beauty and balance.

Shared spaces

A couple's space can be any room. What sets it apart are design elements intended to help two individuals open and share themselves. If you design the space correctly, vulnerable moments can feel safer, heated exchanges can soften and mellow, and cold shoulders can turn into a loving embrace.

A striking combination of feminine softness and masculine strength, this room represents and supports both the masculine and feminine partner. The carved wooden chair next to the plush softness of a slouchy ottoman generates its own yin/yang dynamic, while the paired containers connote a strong coupling. Additionally, some traditional plaid patterns are a complementary combination of yin and yang.

What is wrong with romantic spaces?

If all the "couple spaces" in your home are soft and romantic, that is a good thing, right? Not if one person in the partnership has a strong masculine essence. Essentially what we think of as "romantic" means yin, the feminine side of the partnership. Soft lights, soft colors, soft music, soft textures—it is all yin. These spaces are necessary, since they bring out and support the feminine partner's essence, but they cannot dominate every couple encounter. (Why do you think most masculine guys hang out in the garage instead of in the beautifully decorated soft-flowing living room?)

I would wager that some, if not most, feminine partners would love it if their masculine partner showed more strength, more direction, and more raw primal desire. The feminine partner needs a strong masculine essence in order to fully relax and begin the dance of the feminine. The stronger and more intensely present the masculine partner is, the more completely the feminine partner can experience her flowing gracious nature. But—here is the catch—you cannot expect a strong masculine person to hang out all day in a soft frilly house. That environment will not activate his yang chi force.

Having a hard time figuring out how to make your bedroom peaceful, romantic, and still represent the masculine? How many bedroom sitting areas have you seen that feel like a five-year old's tea party? This bedroom is a lovely restful blend of masculine and feminine, using the energy of two very different yet matching chairs to pull it all together.

Give a guy a leather chair and he is bound to stick around longer.

Use leather. Tried and true, a yang person likes leather. Whether leather activates his primal hunting gene, or some other brain chemical, experience has shown he will be more aggressive on a leather couch than on a couch decorated with a cotton floral print. If you would like to encourage a little more primal play with your partner, add leather.

Incorporating objects that your partner loves will increase his comfort level in the home.

Home cures

What can you do at home? Even though he may not spend as much time at home as you do, he will have a place to land if you incorporate his nature in the home.

Use decor items that represent action and movement. Baseballs, airplanes, and fast cars are all great choices. It is not just that they are traditionally "guy" things, it is that they are fast, and yang chi likes to flow quickly.

Incorporate plaids or squares within squares. The masculine likes to find and emphasize the edge. Although squares are a yin shape, when you put them together in a plaid, they become a symbol of the mathematical, systematic mind. Plaids are not just squares, they are components within a larger system, and any type of "systems thinking" is a masculine activity. Just try wearing a plaid shirt and see how feminine you feel.

De-clutter. I know sometimes it is his "stuff" and not yours that is filling every inch of floor space. However, regardless of whose clutter it is, the more stuff there is in a room, the slower the chi moves. Every stack of paper, every shelf full of knickknacks, all make the room more yin. This is truly a case of less is more—less stuff creates more yang.

A concrete wall lends raw strength to this bedroom, making it a place the masculine would love to frequent. The lamp, pillows, and plants keep it soft enough to appeal to the feminine partner, as well.

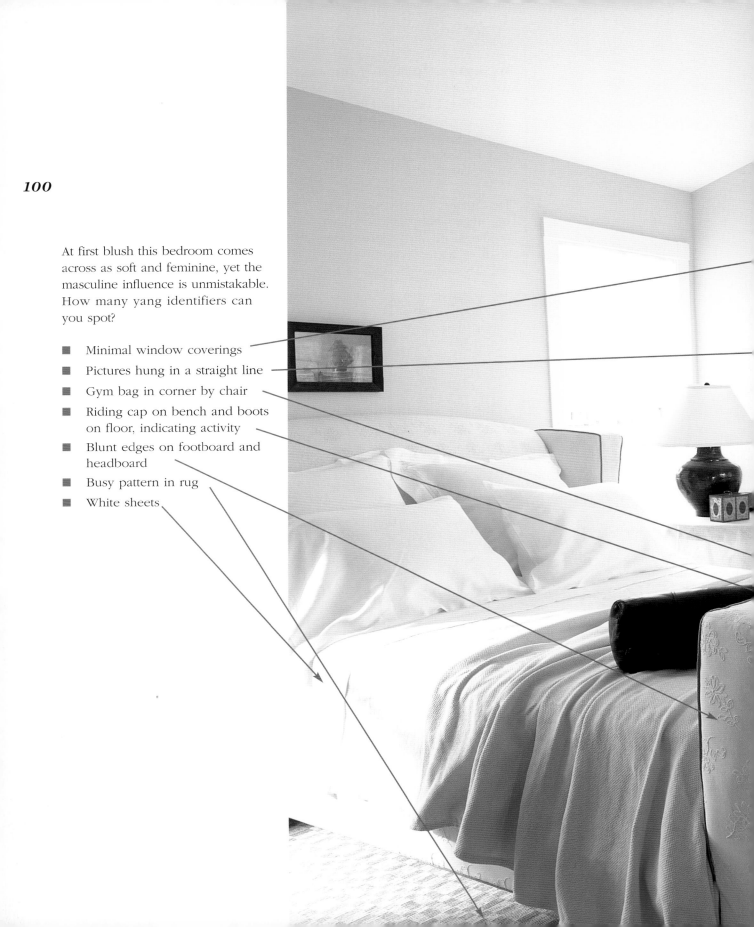

At first blush this bedroom comes across as soft and feminine, yet the masculine influence is unmistakable. How many yang identifiers can you spot?

- Minimal window coverings
- Pictures hung in a straight line
- Gym bag in corner by chair
- Riding cap on bench and boots on floor, indicating activity
- Blunt edges on footboard and headboard
- Busy pattern in rug
- White sheets

According to Christopher Alexander in *A Pattern Language*, ". . . a setting that is full of chairs, all slightly different, immediately creates an atmosphere that supports rich experience; a setting which contains chairs that are all alike puts a subtle straitjacket on experience."

The yin and yang of it

Of primary concern is that both individuals are represented in the space. Nothing shuts a person down faster than to not feel represented in his or her environment. Oftentimes, it is the feminine partner who sets up the couple's entire realm and then wonders why the masculine partner wants nothing to do with it. If a space does not hold enough masculine (what we have been calling "yang") chi, the masculine partner will not feel at home or supported by the space. Since the feminine partner is probably designing and setting up the space, she will need to work with her partner to bring his chi into the room. To create a couple's realm, both partners need to have a say in color selection, furniture selection, and wall decor. Even if he insists he does not care, he will respond better in the space if his needs are considered during the design phase.

Unmatched furniture. Every chair and pillow need not match. In fact, mismatched chairs make it easier for individuals to locate a place in the room that suits them and fits their body. Since women are typically smaller than men, the same chair that feels comfortable to a woman will not support a man. If everything in the space matches, chances are it is suiting only the person who designed it and not accommodating anyone else.

Different moods also require different styles and sizes of chairs. If all your chairs are the same size, what happens when you are in a mood to stretch out and relax vs. curl up into a tight ball?

The photographs in this section were taken to show how messages are communicated through furniture and design. After reading the captions for each photo, think about what kind of caption you would write for each couple's area in your home. Arrange your spaces to invite many more spontaneous moments for two.

The invitation

With the unlimited demands on a person's time today, time together as a couple does not often happen unless it is planned. Unfortunately, it is often spontaneous moments of laughter and sharing that make lasting memories. Cheer up. How you design your room can actually encourage both you and your partner to be more spontaneous. Think of your space design as an invitation. What is it inviting you to do? Do all your seating areas face the TV and not each other? Are your backyard lounge chairs facing the neighbor's garage? Is your bathtub big enough for two? Does your kitchen have enough room for two cooks, instead of one? Do you have pictures up of the two of you interacting in a loving, kind way?

Quiet reflection. **With a serene view of the lake and one chair curved slightly toward the other, this sitting arrangement whispers, "Join me for a moment of quiet reflection."**

Carefree and fun. The fun tropical prints and Mediterranean colors in this sitting area say: "Let's get away somewhere where there's no phone and no family responsibilities."

Wild and wonderful. Your wild side is sure to come out with these daring pillow covers. "Leave your inhibitions at the door!" is the unspoken message here.

Old reliable. Functional and practical, this arrangement is too far away from the fireplace to invite intimacy and the glass and metal table will squelch any spontaneous fun. Its message is more one of cooperation and camaraderie than intimacy and passion. It says, "I'll be here for you when you need my help."

A gathering place—group interactions

Coming together in community is a fundamental human need. In Joseph Campbell's highly acclaimed book, *The Hero with a Thousand Faces*, every life journey begins and ends in community. If you can create a space in your home where people feel accepted, loved, and included, you have performed a great service in the world. Communities come together around common causes. Your common cause might be the same parents or a shared love for jazz. As we all have numerous interests and communities in which we participate, you will have to select your primary communities and keep them in mind when setting up your home's gathering spaces.

Begin with the center in mind. Living rooms and family rooms devoid of the grounding and centering form of a coffee table do not get used. Why is this object in the center so important? In a gathering space, you need to pull disparate energies together and get them to interact. Your central table, ottoman, trunk, or stool accomplishes this by serving as the hub to which the various sitting spokes are attached. This does not mean you are limited to the standard coffee table with a stack of books on top. The following photos illustrate different ways in which to anchor a gathering place.

No stuffy table here. This home owner selected two architectural capitals to create a stunning, as well as grounded, family room.

To balance the ominous weight of the fireplace, this room demanded a large, heavy, stable center. The growing orchids on the table help lift this heaviness, adding some yang life force to an otherwise yin setting.

Try a coffee cart instead of a coffee table. Create your own coffee table out of a novel family heirloom or a yard-sale item. Such pieces appeal to the fun-loving side of us and encourage families to play more together.

Low to the ground, this traditional coffee table needed to be quite large to reach and anchor the different sitting areas around it. Had this table been smaller, the room would not have held together and each sofa or pair of chairs would have felt discon-nected from the center core.

Think in terms of circles

A gathering place needs to wrap around its members and hold them in a circular embrace. Circles represent community energy in numerous cultures including Native American and Asian. It strengthens feelings of inclusion and eliminates separateness. So how do you get the energy in the space to wrap?

Curve seating arrangements. Chairs seated side by side in a nice straight line might pass an army inspection, but they will not make your guests feel like talking to each other. If your furniture is already curved in shape, this point is not as dire. However, for furniture with straight backs and arms, introducing a curve through placement will soften their lines and encourage circular chi motion. Another rule of thumb: Pull furniture out a few inches from the wall and allow chi to circulate behind each piece.

Fill your corners. Empty corners drain energy from the center. Until the corners are full, the center will not feel supported. A carefully placed plant, a pair of five-foot iron candleholders, or a large basket filled with dried bamboo can relieve the stress on the room's center.

This white chair was lost against the white wall. By adding the active red screen, the chair immediately comes to life, beckoning the owner to sit down and snuggle up. As interesting as the screen is, its strongest function in the space is how it wraps energy around the back of the chair.

Implement circular decor items. Circular lamps, rugs, serving bowls, vases, wall art, and tables, all send the subconscious a message of inclusion. Rings (such as a candle with an enclosing candle ring) and wreaths have been used for centuries to signify that even strangers are welcome and that no one is excluded. If you make your wreath out of natural organic materials, it also symbolizes your connection to the seasonal patterns of the natural world and broadens community to include nonhuman forces.

Diversity is the key

Use different-sized chairs. Invite three people over and you will likely have three very different body types in your living room. If each person has to fit into the same size and shape of chair, chances are one or two might be too high, too low, too small, or too soft to be comfortable. Opt for an assortment of chairs, varying the size, shape, and softness of each. The comfort factor of your room increases exponentially.

This natural fir wreath brings the entire stairwell to life, welcoming all who enter. It has marvelous kinetic energy in its whorling branches.

You can bet the child who sits in this green mini Adirondack chair knows he is an accepted, integral part of the family. Make a place for your children as you would for your guests, and they will show up and participate more actively in family interactions.

Incorporate a variety of textures. Just as different-sized chairs increase a sense of comfort and inclusion, multiple textures can also scintillate your guests. A combination of plush carpeting, a linen sofa, and rattan chairs stirs the senses and accommodates the tactile needs of a broad consortium. Try mixing ultramodern textures, such as concrete and crafted steel, with natural components, like jute fibers and carved wood. Shiny silver candlesticks glow even brighter reflected in a rustic wooden mirror, and a silk wall hanging is certain to stand out against a stucco wall.

Cluster three or more together. Whether you are referring to chairs, candles, or coffee-table books, clusters form group energy. When the eye registers a grouping, it expands to "take it all in." Single objects tend to contract the eye (and your chi) in order to focus more fully on that one object.

Although a modern material, the cement wall has been imprinted with a wood-grain texture, which creates a primitive feeling.

Even in this minimalist setting, the owner has clustered seating to generate stronger group energy.

Removing window treatments opened this small living area and revealed a stunning view.

When your gathering place is too small

Use open furniture. Unless you are using a furniture piece to provide storage, keep your selections open and airy so that they do not stop the eye. If you can "see through" a piece, its energetic impact is considerably less than solid pieces.

Use vertical movement. If you cannot spread out, move up. If your ceilings are at least eight feet high, use vertical positioning to create movement for the eye and to lessen the stuck feeling that can settle into a small space. Caution: Avoid placing too many items on furniture or on shelves above your head. Instead of increasing a feeling of freedom, items hanging above the head feel oppressive and threatening.

Minimize window treatments. Heavy drapes will cause the chi to sink. Use vertical coverings or no covering at all to open the space.

Enlarge doorways and openings. Placing decorative items (such as potted plants) on the sides of a doorway can expand the chi of the door, creating more yang movement in the space.

Introduce more living plants. During the day, living plants constantly generate chi, reducing the strain on the human element to fill the space. Emotionally, your home will feel less demanding and more supportive.

By adding a few small tables, an arrangement of flowers, and a basket, this large room becomes more compact.

Size matters

A group gathering is intimately affected by the size of the room. Just as Goldilocks discovered when she went to visit the three bears, group gathering places can be too large, too small, or just right. If yours is just right, lucky you. If not, the following information will give you some tips on how to grow or shrink your space to fit the size of your group.

When your gathering place is too large

Large open spaces seem ideal, but they can drain life force from humans if there is not enough chi present in the surroundings themselves. In a large room, you will have to work harder to make others feel comfortable and included in what is going on.

Increase furniture density. Obviously, the more you fill your space with furniture and decor items, the less "empty" space there is. Be careful not to line your walls and leave the center of your space empty. (See lower photograph on the facing page.)

Watch furniture size. Nothing makes a place feel larger than small furniture items. You are much better off having a few larger pieces than a bunch of small occasional tables or single chairs. Furniture that blocks a view of the wall behind it and the floor beneath it is much more stabilizing in a large space than tables with open legs or shelving that is open to the wall behind it. Open furniture pieces are best in small places.

Too much open space in the center. Connect sitting areas that are further than four feet apart by opting for an L-shaped sofa or adding an ottoman. Central objects allow for a common focal point that connect people to each other.

The ottoman grounds the center of the room, providing a common horizontal surface for all the seating areas.

Add pictures of people. Adding photographs of loved ones, friends, or deceased family members can help you energetically fill a room that would otherwise be too large.

113

This large room is functionally cozy. Here is what makes it work:

- Numerous photographs of family, friends, and travel fill the back table, bringing life to what could otherwise be a dormant area.

- The dark low window edge complemented by the fold in the drapes draws a horizontal line around the room, bringing the energy down to the seating level. This horizontal line also keeps the chi in the room from escaping into the ocean beyond the windows.

- The large L-shaped sofa fills an entire corner. This single piece is much more grounding than scattering numerous small chairs around the room would be.

- The warm earth tones draw energy inward and hold it still, another calming yin feature of the space.

- The variety of textures—smooth wood, supple leather, chenille throw, silk drapes—activate the senses and keep an active energy exchange going throughout the room.

- The strong border around the edge of the rug pulls the room in. The border is more than two feet wide, which draws the items inside it even closer together.

Find that element

This entry hall is a classic balance of all five elements, making it an easy space to greet formal visitors as well as intimate friends. (Remember the elemental nature of an object is discerned by its color, shape, and material.)

- **Earth:** square pictures hung in a horizontal line, cream wall color
- **Metal:** white round Chinese vase, white round pots for plants, metal table stand, clean orderly feeling, gray matting in pictures
- **Water:** cascading plants, black table base with glass tabletop in hallway, privacy aspect of the sliding door (provides more privacy for eating area, which water needs to feel comfortable)
- **Wood:** tall, carved Chinese doors, statues on top of interior wall that raise the eye to the same height as the carved doors, vertical panels in the dining room, hardwood flooring, pillar shapes in table base
- **Fire:** triangular pendulum in table base, red rugs, track lighting to spotlight objects in the evening, brightly colored flowers on the dining table, diamond patterns in the rug

118　The formal living room

Tradition plays a strong role in formal living rooms, symbolizing your link to your ancestral past. Living rooms are more formal spaces than family rooms, and have their own story to tell. Your formal living room is your connection to ancestral energy patterns. Rooted in tradition, the items displayed in your living room reveal your family-of-origin's imprint on your current reality. Our link to the past determines how safe we feel in the present. This living room holds several past-generation items:

- iron mantel brought from the ancestral home,
- wall scrolls that depict the family's history,
- family kimono
- refinished chairs from a prior generation,
- antique wall hangings, trunk, and drum tables.

The family room

The family room or its cousin, the great room, allows for a psychological separation between the ancestral family and the immediate family. The relaxed nature of a family room or great room gives you the space to play and explore, trying out different ways of interacting than you might have grown up with. Family rooms and great rooms often function as the mingling zones, the places where family members come together after exiting their private spaces (bedrooms and offices). As such, the family room needs to hold objects that relate to each family member.

Once every member has adequate "representation," you can work on adding layers of functionality that will combine to make this room a place that does indeed bring your family together. This room holds:

- the husband's favorite wall art,
- the husband's CD collection,
- the wife's cozy throw,
- a child's favorite reading book.

122 Avoid computers in this room. Family rooms are for interactions. Usually, the type of family interaction that happens surrounding a computer is arguing over turns. Computers encourage people to tune into a virtual reality, rather than work to enhance their actual reality. The computer is now the source of more "couple" fights than any other piece of electronic equipment in the house, including the television.

Family rooms that inhibit movement train people to be passive. This passivity can extend to numerous areas of a person's life. If you want your children to be actively involved in making their life decisions, give them the space to move and explore.

Play together. What kind of play does your family engage in? Do you pull out a chess set or play the piano? Do you tell stories or wrestle on the floor? Whatever form of family play suits you, make certain you have the space, the toys, or the props you need to entice interest at a moment's notice.

Invite neighbors and friends into this space often. Help young ones know that their family-of-origin relates harmoniously with larger social patterns. If no one but the family is ever in the family room, children do not get to see how their family fits into the larger social picture.

Color matters. This is not the place for a white-on-white color scheme. Use child- and spill-friendly colors and make certain that at least 60 percent of the colors in the room are warm tones. (See **Which colors are safe?** on pages 224–226.)

Lamplighting. Soft light encourages more intimate conversation, but be certain it is bright enough that people can see the expressions on each others' faces. Much of our communication happens through facial expressions, rather than through spoken words. Candles added to lamplight sprinkle magic throughout family moments and energeti-cally bond family members together.

This relaxed room invites family fun. The ottoman on wheels can be rolled away to open the center, allowing room for wild and rambunctious children to play.

Include a mantel. A mantel is not only an important focal point, it is a strong indicator of ability to attract chi. Linked to the ancestral hearth, a fireplace does not need to be lit to attract chi. An interesting and purposeful mantel arrangement can bring the energetic patterns of various shapes to work for you, gathering chi. Empty fireplaces should be avoided at all costs, since they represent dormancy and the inability to bring potential possibilities into the realm of the actual.

The reverse triangle created by these two horses set amidst the wall sconces is a way of directing power (chi force) down from heaven into the house.

The environmental interior

There are many ways of bringing the powerful influence of nature indoors. Regardless of whether or not you enjoy a year-round porch, you can select one of your favorite places in nature as a decorating theme. When you create an interior tribute to the seashore, a pine forest, or a woodland meadow, you create a home space that resonates with a particular natural environment. The effect is more than visual. Your home's frequency alters. If selected as your theme, the jungles of the rain forest, for example, would influence your senses, thought patterns, and emotional responses. The truer you are to your natural source of inspiration, the stronger this energetic link will be. For many it is a sacred connection.

It is not hard to imagine yourself on safari when you walk into this sitting room. Palm trees, antelope-patterned rug, tropical-print chaise lounge, and bamboo chairs all work together to bring this adventurous room to life.

Capture color

The strongest visual and vibratory link to your natural environment is color. Even with no ocean view, a periwinkle/white combo invites the seashore into your home while fuchsia pink lands you in the middle of a tropical island. The warm glow of terra-cotta walls can recall a walk down a path of sun-baked earth, and celadon green holds the allure of an Asian dynasty.

The color-capturing process is where all your magazine reading can come in handy. Rip out pictures of places that resonate with your theme and match them up with paint chips. Try buying quarts of various "theme" colors and mixing them on the wall, layering your gold over your green until you get just the right hue. This eliminates the stress of painting the entire room only to realize that your "palladian blue" looks mint green or that a soft violet turned gray. Once you get just the right color mixed on your wall (and in your paint tray), dab a stir stick into the mixture and take it down to a paint specialist that hand-mixes color. Computer matching is rarely close enough for energy design.

Materials

Stone. As a bowl of pebbles, a heart-shaped stone next to an intimate photo, a rock garden, or a slab for a coffee table, stone enters the home in many ways. Cobblestone paths will teleport you all the way to old Europe, so why not use two cobblestones as bookends? If you pick up favorite rocks on a nature walk, add them to a zen sand garden for a dynamic effect. If river rocks are your favorite, why not refinish your family-room mantel with your private collection?

Tile. Mexico comes instantly to mind with its deep blue and terra-cotta tiles. France has its own tile style, opting for white-and-blue scrollwork or a crisp black-and-white check, and the red roofs of Spain strike even the casual visitor. Tile can hang on the wall like a photo, deck out your floor, or rest in a tabletop. A tile trivet works in the kitchen and tile borders can be added almost anywhere. Glazed tiles increase yang, adding movement to the room, whereas unglazed tiles are porous and absorbent, increasing yin.

Wood. Wood is one of the most fundamental building blocks of any environment and can take the form of a bark basket, a hollowed-out stump for a planter, a carved mirror frame, or an antique door. Avail yourself of wood and you capture the strength of its original location.

Wicker. This bending reed can take almost any shape, indicating flexibility and endurance. Wicker is also a strong summer signal (See **Seasons** on page 128.) and beach locator. It is hard to walk along a string of beach houses anywhere in the world and not see wicker in some form. No room for a wicker rocking chair? Try a floor basket or a small table.

This carved-wood table evokes a sense of faraway places. The wicker chair helps support the feeling that this room is a retreat from chaos.

Metal. Scrolls, braces, table legs, and lamps—metal is easy to add. Lending its edge to ancient civilizations as well as to modern lofts, metal provides the ability to define a space, carving out the area surrounding an object in order to add clarity. This clarity can feel sharp if overdone. Soften metal's sharp edges by surrounding it with an absorbent material such as wood.

Leather. Full of fire, leather brings the animation and life of the animal kingdom into a physical environment. It is no wonder that leather brings out the masculine life force in people, putting most men instantly at ease in a room. Leathers range from rough Montana cowhides to supple Italian pieces, with everything in between. Studded leather couches, pincushion stools, or coffee-table inlays, all increase the yang energy in a room as well as heighten sensitivity to touch.

Cut glass, like this round, faceted crystal, can bring rainbow rays into the room.

Glass. What else can create rainbows on your wall, protect you from the eyes of prying neighbors, or allow you to feel the warmth of the sun on a winter's day? Glass is multi-faceted. It can be transparent or opaque, thick or thin, clear or colored. A wall of glass blocks can modernize a blasé rambler with the updated feel of a city loft. An antique glass collection can land you back on an ancestral farm.

Woven fibers and textiles. A brilliant turquoise-blue pashmina throw from India can make any room feel exotic. This wonderful combination of silk and wool gets softer with every washing, and is as functional as it is beautiful. Old cottons, denims, or a patchwork quilt made from flannel pajamas will support your effort to create a rustic getaway, just as velvet is sure to come across as posh and luxurious. Woven fibers and textiles are as tactile as they are visual. Be certain to take into account what you will touch, as well as what you will see.

Scents

A powerful link, smell should be considered a part of your decorating scheme, rather than an afterthought. Every home has particular scents that are the accumulation of the various activities and objects in the home. Be certain to refresh sensory experiences often, keeping them in harmony with the seasons.

Seasons

Capture the best season of your selected environment. If you visit the Rocky Mountains during ski season, your tribute to this mountain environment should include a snowy landscape or antique wooden skis. If your trips to the seashore are your favorite summer outing, your seashore room might be painted the sandy color of driftwood bleached by the sun. Many furnishings have seasonal associations. Bamboo suggests the quick growth of spring, wicker evokes summer, a leaf motif recalls the fall, and leather summons winter. If the environment you are working with does not experience strong seasonal changes, you can still shift the color of your flowers, candles, or coverings to keep your home feeling alive.

The skis, plaid furnishings, and roaring fire bring back strong memories of a winter spent skiing in the Rockies.

Thematic objects

Let your travels be your guide. Environmental interiors are stronger if they link to a place you have personally experienced. It is nice to do the log cabin theme, but if you have never inhaled the crisp, cold, pine-scented air of a Rocky Mountain December or chopped wood for a morning fire, then your link to that environment will not be as strong. When selecting a theme, consider special childhood places, favorite romantic getaways, or travels to other cultures. If you were to sit down, close your eyes, and call up a "place in nature" that would make you feel both comfortable and alive; that place should be your theme environment. The objects should have a spiritual aesthetic that can breathe soul into the room.

Recreate your favorite vacation just by using colors and collected objects from the locale in your decor.

Outdoor living spaces

The constancy of change

A blur of green. The smell of grass. A profusion of color. Warm evening air. Outdoor environments have their own magic, their own finesse. To be outside is to interface with nature spirits and the souls of trees, as well as city streets and neighboring fences. Somewhere between the urban and the primitive, outdoor spaces open us and soothe us like no indoor space can.

Comfortable outdoor spaces evolve as you learn to interact with the natural forces that make up your landscape. Whether those forces include trees, boulders, hills, rich soil, clay, blue jays, or skyscrapers, you must create a relationship in which you communicate your needs to nature and learn to listen to her replies.

Feng shui is the study of how the natural patterns of the environment interface with and affect human beings. The first thing to consider about an outdoor environment is that you necessarily give up quite a bit of control. You do not control the temperature, or whether it is intensely bright or dark and cloudy. You cannot keep pests away, or airborne seeds. From the minute you wake up in the morning to the time you go to bed, your outdoor environment is changing. The more you plan for those changes, the easier it is to transform them into a source of enrichment rather than frustration.

I go to nature to be soothed and healed, and to have my senses put in order.

—John Burroughs

A comfortable outdoor environment is one that works with, not against, natural patterns and forces.

An outdoor trellis is a yin feature, adding elements of protection, shade, and support.

Tempering with yin and yang

Every day, the morning sun dries the dew from the grass, wakes up the birds, and floods the sky with color. The yang increases. Each evening sun pulls all those glorious colors back in, waves goodbye with a wink, and then is gone. Yin increases. Yang's force is felt as spring pushes tender flowers up through crusty snow and summer blazes wilt flowers in a day. Yin's softening begins in the fall, toning everything back down, settling into the deep yin of winter. Outdoor designers must learn to balance the yin and yang shifts of nature to create spaces that allow us to enjoy a fullness of outdoor experiences. When the sun dims in the evening, the outdoor gazebo glows with twinkling lights. When the sun blazes white hot, we pull a stretch of canvas across a frame to create shade. We temper wind with trees, add rocks to create visual interest during winter, and find ways to keep flowers blooming from early spring to late fall.

Yin features. Yin garden features provide safety, shelter, and relaxation. They tend to decrease the human element and increase the natural element. For example, a garden bench overgrown with ivy would be more yin than the same bench in the center of a patio with no ivy in sight. Hanging plants are more yin than upright ones, and any item that brings the eye or body down lower to the ground will increase yin. Yin surfaces are often soft and absorbent, since the nature of yin is to receive energy and hold it still.

Yang features. Yang garden features invite exploration, activity, and movement. They allow the sun free reign and provide plenty of reflective surfaces to keep the light bouncing. Bright colors, patterns, and dynamic shapes are all a part of yang's array. Harder surfaces will keep energy moving faster than absorbent ones, as will straight lines. And any upright vertical object such as a tall tree, birdhouse, or sundial keeps chi moving up and out in a yang pattern.

Adding a vertical object to an overgrown (and, therefore, yin) flower bed area will increase yang.

Between haven and earth

A gradual transition between outside and inside is essential for harmony between your home and its surroundings. When grass runs directly to the walls of the house, the connection between earth and home is too abrupt. A transition space where outdoors and indoors mix is needed. Home owners without a transition space may feel cut off from the world, unable to connect intimately to family, friends, and nature.

■ Shrubs, flower beds, and other forms of greenery should rise up to meet the house. Higher than the surrounding lawn, greenery will ground the house, making it feel safe and rooted in the earth. Without this semienclosure in Mother Earth, a house feels out of place, transplanted, and unsafe.

- A curved path to the house encourages visitors to slow their approach and shift more gradually from outdoors to in.
- Porches create the perfect interface; they function somewhat like a room, providing relief from sun and elements, and somewhat like a yard, full of plants and sunshine.
- Rock gardens are great outdoor features for high-altitude environments that do not allow long growth cycles. Like shrubs or bushes, rocks can ground and stabilize a house, helping it feel solid, permanent, and safe.

This owner used rock quarried from the surrounding hillside to link her yard to the grounding, stabilizing force of an entire mountain.

Protective porches

136 A porch is a wonderful potpourri of experience. Structurally, it represents shelter and protects one from exposure to the elements. By definition, a porch is a covered vestibule, but when the vestibule is uncovered, then it is not able to perform this protective function. You and your visitors will feel vulnerable. If your porch is exposed, place an item there that signals your willingness to care for yourself and your visitors. This could be a welcome sign, welcome mat, a bench to set items down on, or even a colorful pot of flowers.

Front porches. Because the front porch is attached to the face of the house, it provides the ornament for the front door, and as such, signals the wealth status and social position of the inhabitants. For example, the long porches of the Arts and Crafts bungalows were associated with financial misfortune during the depression (often called poverty porches) because the men who were laid off and out of work would hang out on the porch all day. Also, porches that were exposed underneath (meaning that someone could access the ground underneath the porch) were risking their fortunes. Use lattice or wooden planks to close off any access to the ground underneath the porch. Keep the porch freshly painted or varnished and remove any sign of neglect (cobwebs in the corners, etc.). Make certain that your porch does not look dormant during winter months.

Color is a simple way to welcome visitors. This cheery yellow porch invites guests to relax and enjoy the moment.

Back porches/decks. A large back porch or deck is especially important for men, as it provides a transition space between the house and the outside world where they can feel connected to the goings-on inside the house without actually being inside. Women use the back porch or deck to access the wilder, less public aspects of their psyches. If the back deck is exposed to neighbors in the rear, both men and women will feel vulnerable.

A protective lattice creates a private sanctuary out of an otherwise exposed deck.

The meandering path

Paths do much more than direct guests to your front door. Paths create mystery and wonder. As they curve out of sight or lead up to a gate, they suggest that there is more, much more, to be discovered.

A path is a journey. The paths you create influence what type of journey yours will be. Will it be fast or slow? Will the purpose of the journey be reaching the end or walking the path? In evaluating your property's paths, consider the following features:

- materials,
- relationship to nature,
- destination.

Materials. Grass, dirt, wood, brick, flagstone, rock, cement. This materials list is organized beginning with the most yin materials and ending with the most yang. The more yang your materials are, the more the emphasis shifts to control over the natural.

Relationship to nature. How you place your materials also influences how yin or yang it is. The path itself is the yang element, representing the human influence over nature. The surrounding environment or space between path elements is nature's yin influence. Stones placed close together would create a hard yang path, but the same stones placed far enough apart to allow for the grass to grow up between them is much more yin. Too much yin nature can overwhelm the yang human element, however, creating blocks on one's journey.

The grass between the stones on this path subdues the human element and increases yin.

Destination. When destinations are clearly visible from the path, the focus becomes the destination, rather than the journey. Increase the sense of mystery in your life by arranging for surprises that unfold at the end of a path, such as this seating arrangement. If the size of your yard does not allow for such surprises, delight yourself along the way by adding other whimsies such as flowering moss between stones or a unique collection of stones.

Place something at the end of your path to strengthen a sense of arrival. This secret meeting area is well worth the journey.

This sunny seat is the perfect place to spend the morning.

When a stone bench is warmed by the sun, it becomes both supportive and energizing.

A "sit" spot

Take nature's daily cycles into account when deciding where to place sitting areas. You will need more than one sitting area to accommodate the position of the sun at different times of day. The minimum for outdoor comfort is a shady spot for easing outside in the morning, a bright sunny spot to get warm, and a cool-down area for sunsets at the end of the day. Where you place your morning and late-afternoon rest zones will depend on the shade provided by neighboring houses and surrounding trees, but keep the following feng shui wisdom in mind as well.

Morning seating areas. These need to support your visionary side (grand vistas are good here). The beginning of the day is related to the Wood element in feng shui and is best suited for envisioning new projects, planning your daily activities, or brainstorming novel solutions to old problems. As such, you should locate your morning sitting area where you feel expansive and have a view of the sky (can you recline your seat?). The sky represents uncharted territory, the realm of discovery and unlimited potential. Use your piece of sky to think outside your normal realm.

Adding an umbrella to your table gives you more control over the elements and allows the same area to serve you during different times of day.

Late afternoon seating areas. Here is a place for ingathering everything that was scattered during the day. As such, these areas are best placed next to a pool of water where the energy of the water itself can help you draw yourself back in.

Water invites reflection and slows the physical body, preparing it for a time of rest. If you cannot sit next to a pond or hot tub, use the power of metal to help you collect your thoughts. Metal creates dense, concentrated energy patterns that will help you pull everything together and make sense out of the whole. Metal also represents refinement and letting go of anything that is out of harmony with your essence, and will help you to release anything toxic that you are holding in your energy field. When it comes to the end of the day, think small cozy spots.

Full-sun seating areas. Although these areas are too intense in the middle of the day and/or middle of the summer, they provide a necessary yang influence during more yin times of the year. A fall afternoon might be too cool in the shade, but the warmth of the sun is just enough to melt aching muscles and relax the entire body. Related to the fire element, full-sun areas are about letting go of the past and being fully present in the moment. It is ideal to have a lounger chair that you can lie down on and close your eyes in order to bring your consciousness 100 percent to the physical experience of total relaxation. You will not need a plug-in for your laptop here. Letting go, not productivity, is the purpose of this space.

This rounded gate captures a magical view of the side yard, creating a sense of wonder and discovery.

A framed view

No matter how small your yard, you can still create pleasant views. The necessary element for a view is a frame to contain it. There are many different types of frames; but the frame, more than the actual view, determines the effect.

I never saw an ugly thing in my life: for let the form of an object be what it may—light, shade, and perspective will always make it beautiful.
—John Constable

To frame your views, take your camera outside. Looking around your yard through the lens will help you locate your most inspiring views. Once you have located them, you can frame them by:

- positioning sitting areas to capture a particular view;
- trailing ivy or shaping the growth of surrounding plants;
- installing a lattice, arch, or arbor;
- placing stepping stones to lead the eye down a path;
- cutting away existing shrubbery, hedges, or trees;
- elevating your view by building a deck or raised patio.

A way with water

To the Chinese, water is money. Even the English word abundance, which comes from the Latin word *abundare*, literally means to overflow. Water brings the energy patterns of flow, abundance, and ease to one's life. However, putting in a pond or pool is trickier than you might think. The shape, placement, and condition of the pool all affect whether your fortunes increase or diminish. If you decide to add a water feature to your yard, keep the following feng shui tips in mind.

Choose the right shape. Water does not flow in straight lines, so a straight-sided pool will not generate the same energy patterns that a curved one will. Irregular shapes imply flexibility and movement, straight lines imply control and strength. If you swim to feel free and relax, a kidney-shaped pool will help. If you swim to feel strong and in control of your life, a rectangular-shaped pool is great for you.

Embrace the house. Position your pool or pond so that it curves toward the house, embracing it, rather than bending away from the house. The inside curve is where chi builds, the outside edge is constantly losing chi. Curve your pool in to hold your chi.

A small bamboo spout has abundant ways to comfort and soothe with water.

This kidney-shaped pool encourages fluidity and relaxation.

Ba gua map

Abundance	Fame/ reputation	Intimate relations
Family/ ancestors	Health	Children/ creativity
Self knowledge	Journey/ career	Helpful people

Entrance

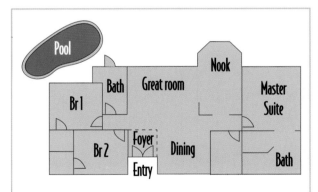

Use the pool to balance the house. If your house is missing any areas of the ba gua map, place the pool in the missing area. Because pools and ponds hold tremendous life force, this feature can bring vitality and chi to an otherwise dormant area of your yard (and your life).

Place the pool according to the ba gua. The ancient template, or map, that balances the energy that flows through a home or yard is called the ba gua. According to this map, some areas benefit from increased Water while others lose energy. The best places for a pool or pond are the front-center section of your yard (the Journey/career sector) and the rear-left section (relating to wealth and Abundance).

Stabilize a pool in the Fame area of the ba gua. Avoid placing a water feature in the Fame/reputation area of your yard (rear center). This area relates to Fire energy, which has an upward, expansive dynamic, the opposite of downward-flowing water. A pond in Fame can create "damp" conditions for the heart and also dampen your reputation. If your pond or pool is already situated in the Fame area, balance the downward flow with a sprinkler head that shoots water directly up into the air and add large rocks to stabilize the volatile combination of Water and Fire.

Integrate the pool with its natural surroundings. The most interesting thing about money is that those who do not feel comfortable with it cannot seem to hold on to it. Time and again, people who acquire large sums of money quickly lose it just as quickly. They do not know how to integrate the energy of money into their lives. It feels unnatural and alien to their personal chi and, as a result, their interaction with it is brief. Since your water feature represents your psychological ability to gather and accumulate money, you want it to appear as a natural part of your home and life. It should look as if it has been there for centuries.

144

Make certain the liner does not leak. Most plastic liners will leak over time, and digging everything out to fix it is a monumental task. To the Chinese, leaking pools connote impending bankruptcy and financial disaster. You might want to consider the leakproof fiberglass form. These forms come in numerous shapes, depths, and sizes.

Keep the water clean. Most of us intend to put in a pond and end up with a swamp. Consider using a natural cleaning agent that will cleanse the water. Since water represents your financial situation, you do not want it murky. If you need some grime in the pond, for koi or other fish to feed from, be certain to keep a low pump running to balance it out.

Avoid disappearing-edge pools. The illusion of water, and by association money, flowing over the edge into the abyss is not auspicious. You need to visually contain the water to hold on to the money. If you already have a disappearing edge, plant trees on the other side to create a visual boundary and strengthen the sense of containment.

Replace any fish that die. The cultural significance of dead fish in China is noteworthy. The Chinese believe that any *shar* chi (negative, intense energy) can be absorbed by the fish in a pond, and that the fish willingly takes this chi in to protect its owner. If the fish dies, thank it for its generosity and assistance and replace it as soon as possible.

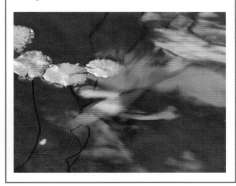

As beautiful as this pond is, care must be taken to clean it regularly, otherwise it will generate a stagnant energy field that will affect the owner's financial status.

Ba gua fundamentals

When we align ourselves with the natural energy patterns of the universe, things flow more smoothly. When we do not, we place ourselves in resistance to the natural ways of things.

For thousands of years, Chinese have studied what happens to energy as it flows through a space. They have discovered a predictable pattern between different physical locations in your home and different aspects of your life. They discovered that a certain part of your home relates directly to your personal abundance, another to career, and another to intimate relationships, for example. If a part of the home is missing, no energy flows to that aspect of life. On the other hand, if part of the home receives a lot of energy and attention, that area of life blossoms. This map of how energy flows through a physical space is called the ba gua. To bring harmony and balance into your life, align the energy in your home to the energetic patterns represented by the different sectors of the ba gua. To do this, you first need to map the ba gua onto your home so you know which areas of your home relate to which sectors.

Are you passionate about what you do for a living?

When you go to work, do you feel a sense of internal alignment, as if you were marshaling your energies together to focus them on the task in front of you? If not, which part of your body is in resistance?

Do you feel that something is preventing you from trying new things?

Do you feel that anything is possible for you to accomplish?

Do you feel like your life has purpose and that it gives you the opportunity to give your deepest gifts in the world?

Journey (career)

Journey is the beginning point of your life. It holds energy of the womb, winter, midnight, and gestation. Associated with the water element (represented in this room by the blue walls), this is the great mother from which all life springs. This energy is unbounded, infinite, open to the ends of consciousness and beyond. This sector is often referred to as the career sector because it also governs our beliefs about what we feel we can accomplish in the world.

How much time do you spend alone? Do you welcome it?

What kinds of things do you like to do alone?

Do you feel like there is enough time, money, or energy for your personal growth? If not, what are your energy drains?

When you get extra time or money, what do you spend it on? What needs are you trying to fill?

Do you feel that your boundaries are clearly defined? Do others often overstep?

Do you wear black or a combination of black and white often? If so, are strong boundaries important to you?

Self-knowledge (wisdom)

The energy pattern of Self-knowledge begins your emergence from the watery womb of Journey. Associated with the elements of earth and the mountain, this sector represents the process of individuation. This process involves setting clear boundaries and distinguishing your personal needs. As the mountain, you must learn to be still, centered, grounded, and feel your own strength. A single item, such as this chair, is a reminder to turn inward.

Do you have a tendency to hold on to things from the past that serve no purpose now?

Are you the storekeeper of the family heirlooms? If you are, the chi in this sector might be stagnant.

Do you display photographs of your family members? Are any members missing from your photograph collection?

Are there objects in your home that remind you of where you grew up? How do you feel about those objects?

Have you kept things that your parents gave you? What kind of energy do those objects hold?

When you look at things you created as a child, what empowered you to create them? What restrained you?

Family Heritage

The Family Heritage gua helps you learn about yourself within the context of a family. This gua holds the accumulated power of those who came before you and provides opportunities for your continued growth. The energy in this area holds the ambitions, dreams, desires, habits, and beliefs of parents, siblings, and ancestors. These energies are a part of your personal path, whether you acknowledge their influence or not. Associated with the wood element, they form the trunk of the tree from which you grow.

Are you happy with your financial situation? If not, where would you like it to be?

Do you make, but also spend, a lot of money? Is there not enough to start with? Is there enough for what you want to do? Are you passionate about what you do every day? Do you feel you can bring your all to it? Is your chosen career in alignment with your life's purpose?

In which areas of your life do you feel abundant? Do you have a lot of time?

Do you have a rich social life and close friends? Rewarding relationships with children?

Do you have a naturally sunny disposition? A keen analytical mind? A sense for fashion? An ability to help others communicate?

Abundance (wealth)

As you align yourself with your life's purpose, you begin to feel more full of Abundance. Governed by the wind element and the color purple, this gua represents the opening up of energy that is always present. The wind brings us all we need. Our task is to open to its blessings. The energy of Abundance encourages us to be ourselves, to live our dreams, and give our gifts. This gua is associated with material wealth. Though money can facilitate the pursuit of dreams, focusing on money often prevents us from seeing other forms of abundance. By acknowledging the numerous manifestations of Abundance, our relationship with money often changes.

What would you like someone to recognize you for? How would they show you that they value you?

Is there anyone in your life who sees and appreciates what you do?

Do you feel visible?

Do you feel like you have something valuable to offer the world?

Do you feel comfortable dancing, yelling, or in other ways extending yourself in the company of others?

Fame (external recognition)

As you give your gifts joyfully, the world recognizes your efforts. This Fame sector is where you shine. It gives the world a way to say thank you and to affirm that what you are doing in your life is important. This recognition is not always in the form of awards. It can be cards from friends or drawings from children. Fame is governed by the fire element, which is enhanced by the triangular-shaped window in this photograph and associated with symbols of transformation.

152

Are you in an intimate relationship? If so, are you happy in that relationship? Do you trust your partner and do you feel trustworthy?

How do you feel about your relationship with mother earth? Have you incorporated patterns into your life that support and nurture the earth, such as recycling, composting, minimal waste, and sustainable living?

Do you feel connected to something larger than yourself?

When you make a commitment to a person or a project, do you follow through with it? Do you allow yourself to receive help from others?

Intimate Relationships (commitment)

The Intimate Relationships gua encourages you to develop relationships of trust, openness, and mutual support. Ruled by the earth element, this area is dedicated to your connection with mother earth. It represents your ability to make a commitment to something greater than yourself (a career, a home, the earth, or another person) and your openness and willingness to allow others to support and nurture you.

Are you excited
about life?

Are you full of
curiosity and
wonder?

Do you make time
to play and relax?

Do you enjoy
your free time?

If you have
children, are they
imaginative in
their play and
positive in their
outlook?

How do you
express your
creative energy?

Are you able to
focus on a given
task and bring it
to completion?

Creative Offspring (children)

This gua is the playground of childhood. The natural result of receiving supportive and nurturing energy from an intimate other is a burst of creative energy. Sometimes this energy manifests in the birth of children, sometimes in other creative projects. Whether you have children or not, everyone needs an area to play, explore, create, and destroy. Do not take yourself or the world too seriously. This sector is related to the metal element, and pulls energy inward to a focal point. This inward movement generates the dynamics necessary to give birth to new creations, especially to create intellectual ideas.

Can you name five people who function as teachers, benefactors, or mentors in your life?

Are you currently functioning as a mentor to someone? How do you feel in that role?

How often do you extend yourself beyond your family?

What communities do you participate in? Business associations? Religious groups? Common interest groups? Men's or women's groups? Travel groups? If you were to open more fully to a sense of community, what type of people would you want to spend more time with?

Do you communicate with spirit guides? Activating this gua will encourage them to play a more active role in your life.

Helpful People (community)

The end of the life cycle is a time of sharing your gifts with a spouse, your children, and the entire community. Governed by the metal element (all the circles in this photograph represent metal), this sector helps draw together the various parts of your life's story. This area of your home symbolizes your connection to a universal life force, your visible and invisible means of support, and your sense of community. This cosmic energy encourages you to call for aid from spiritual communities and heavenly beings, as well as physical neighbors. This gua is connected to travel.

Do you wake up feeling energetic and ready to start the day?

Do you get colds often or take longer than anticipated to heal?

Does life feel stressful and overwhelming?

Do your children have too little or too much energy?

Do you feel that your eating and exercise habits are in alignment with your spiritual goals?

Have you had any major health problems surface since you moved into your house?

Health

At the center of the home, the Health sector is where the energies of all the other sectors combine and balance. It should be open and free from walls, furniture, or hallways. The Health sector is governed by the earth element, representing your ability to nurture and support yourself. Your physical body lets you know when you are out of balance. This sector encourages you to be in your body, listen to its voice, and bring its needs into balance with the rest of your life.

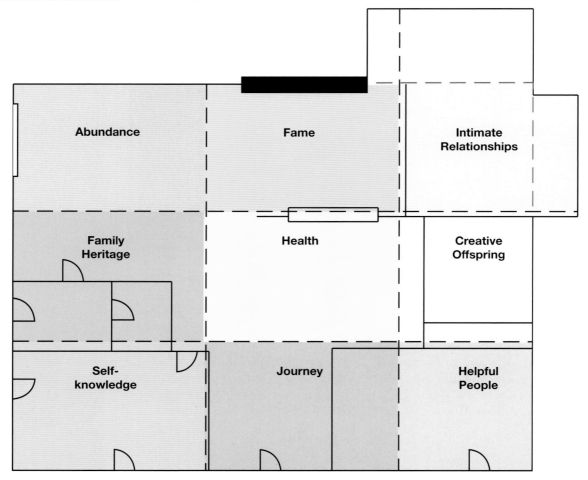

The front door serves as the face of the house, the transition space between the chi of the environment and the chi of the house.

Applying the ba gua to your home

The ba gua is positioned according to "the mouth of chi." For an entire home, the mouth of chi is the architectural front door (where the house numbers are displayed), even if you use a side entrance, back entrance, or garage entrance more than you do the front door. Position the ba gua map so that the front door is either aligned with the Self-knowledge, Journey, or Helpful People sectors. To do this, go outside and stand facing the house. If your front door is on the left side of the house, then you enter your space through the Self-knowledge sector. If the front door is in the middle of the house, you enter into Journey. And if the front door is on the right side, you enter into Helpful People. These three guas form the front line of the ba gua (sometimes referred to as the Kan line). Assuming that the house is rectangular, the rear right corner will be Intimate Relationships, the rear middle gua is Fame, and the rear left gua is Abundance.

Abundance	Fame	Intimate Relationships
Family Heritage	Health	Creative Offspring
Self-knowledge	Journey	Helpful People

The ba gua lays over your floor plan as a template. The front door usually falls in either the Self-knowledge, Journey, or Helpful People sector.

Irregularly shaped houses create projections or enhancements, depending on the size of the extension. Typically, an imbalance in the structural design of the house corresponds with an imbalance in how the person experiences life.

Mapping irregularly shaped houses

Not every house is a perfect rectangle. Irregularly shaped houses create shifts in energy, pulling in more here and allocating less there. These shapes need not create missing sectors. Sometimes the shape creates a projection, or enhancement, of one sector, rather than a missing piece of another. In general, if the existing portion is at least half the width of the house, it has enough density to pull energy in on the other side of the house, thus creating a missing piece. If the existing portion is less than half, it projects energy outward, but does not create an inward pull. Therefore, the piece is projection and there is nothing missing.

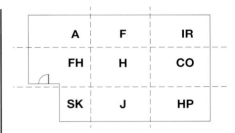

A	F	IR
FH	H	CO
SK	J	HP

A missing sector distorts the natural pattern and cuts off the flow of energy to those life aspects associated with the missing sector.

A slanted wall reducing a sector requires special attention. Place an energizing object such as a plant or lamp in the corresponding sector of a room that relates to the missing sector.

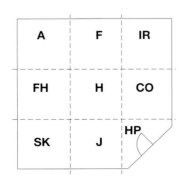

A	F	IR
FH	H	CO
SK	J	HP

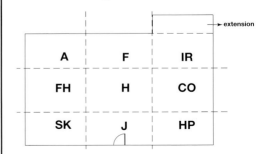

→ extension

A	F	IR
FH	H	CO
SK	J	HP

An enhancement may result in the abundance of energy in an area. More chi flows into the area associated with the related life aspect.

Floor plans

General features. This floor plan incorporates the best of two worlds, the closed doors and private spaces of the Victorian era with the wide open plains of the west. The blending of open spaces, where energy can flow, and smaller closed spaces, where energy can slow down and rest, help balance the yin and yang. Almost every room has natural light on two sides, increasing the overall chi flow and usability of the space.

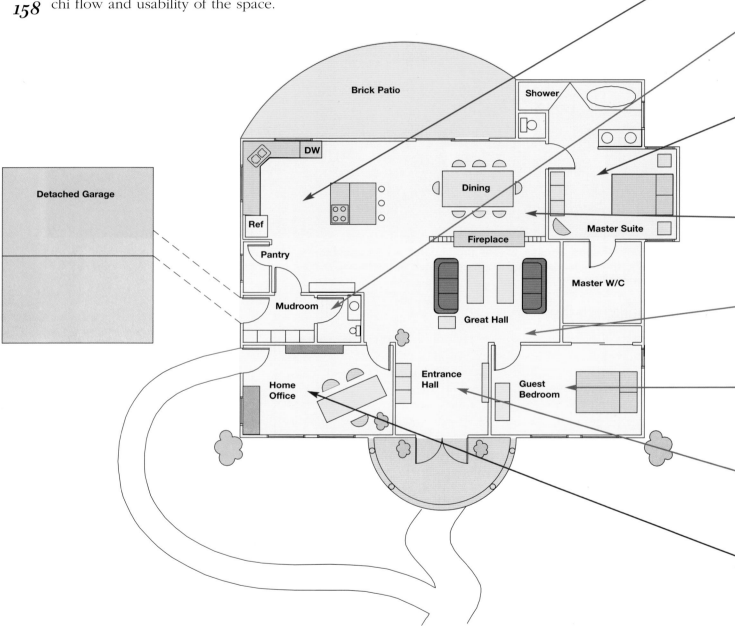

A good floor plan draws together many auspicious features and design details without creating problems for the inhabitants.

Kitchen. The kitchen provides an intimate association between the cook and family/guests. The island is two heights, a lower level for cooking and a higher level for bar seating. The wrap-around windows provide a restful view from the sink and create an active chi flow in the Abundance sector of the house. Fire and water elements have ample space in between.

Mudroom/guest bath. As the primary entrance into the house from the garage, the mudroom provides a transition space between the outside world and the private realm. Equipped with built-in storage cubbies and a bench for removing shoes and outdoor gear, this earthy room with tile floor and thick walls helps people decompress and release stress before coming fully into the house. The guest bath is placed next to this room to stabilize the downward flow of chi present in any bathroom. The two bathrooms on the main floor are totally separate from each other, which stabilizes chi flow throughout the house.

Master suite. The main-floor placement in the back half of the house makes this master suite ideal, eliminating the need to navigate stairs, while providing privacy and quiet. Located in the Intimate Relationships sector of the house, the bath area extends energy outside the outline of the rest of the house. This extension repeats on the right side of the room, providing an abundant energy flow for intimacy. Windows are positioned to the sides of the bed instead of directly behind the headboard, maintaining a stable chi while sleeping. Moving other items, such as a TV or computer, out of the bedroom promotes deeper intimacy. The toilet area is visually separated from the rest of the space. The solid wall prevents views of the bedroom from the patio area. Plenty of closet space is provided to keep things well-organized and keep storage out of the bedroom.

Dining. The dining area enjoys the intimacy of the fireplace and the open freedom of the outdoor patio. The sliding doors to the patio let light in to the back half of the house, keeping chi from stagnating. Separate from the great hall because of the fireplace wall, this room can feel formal or casual, depending on the lighting. Located in the Fame area of the ba gua, the dining area is ideal for entertaining and socializing.

Great hall. This open center room balances the different energies that flow through the various ba gua sectors promoting good health. The glass block wall on both sides of the fireplace, between the great hall and the dining room, blocks energy from passing straight through from the front door out the back patio doors, while allowing natural light into the center of the house. The sidetable by the couch blocks the chi from the front door from hitting the seating area.

Guest bedroom. As a haven for Helpful People, the guest room is self-contained and placed in front of the midline of the house. The bed is placed with the headboard to a solid wall and windows are on the side. With a door opening onto the great room, guests are close to the center of the home without actually being in the middle. The closet provides a sound barrier and additional privacy for the master bedroom. A narrow vertical window to the side of the bed brings light into the other side of the room and keeps chi flowing smoothly. This room could be used as a child's bedroom.

Entrance hall. A winding path leads chi up to the welcoming double doors. The modern, curved porch is anchored with wooden pillars to generate prominence and draw in chi from heaven (good luck chi). The pillars do not to block the view of the door itself. A separate path encourages chi to flow around the side of the house to the home office. The entrance hall is wide and has a bench where guests can remove shoes. Plants ease the transition from the entrance hall into the living areas.

Home office. Placed in the front half of the house, this office is both accessible to visitors and still somewhat separate from the private areas of the home. Visitors enter the office from a side door. Located in the Journey and Self-knowledge area of the ba gua, this room encourages attention to work and inner wisdom. The desk is positioned to provide a view of both doors, with solid walls behind the chair. The windows are placed to the side, providing light and keeping energy moving. A small side window on the left balances out energy on both sides of the room.

Enhancing ba gua sectors

If you find that you have a section missing in your home, or that a sector does not receive as much energy as you would like it to, you can restore balance by directing energy to that area. For the adjustments to be as effective as possible, follow the processes outlined for each adjustment below; but feel free to substitute adjustment items that resonate with your lifestyle, your experiences, and your cultural and personal symbolism.

General adjustments. Depending on your situation, you might need to adjust for a missing sector either outside or inside the house. If you are living in an apartment, for example, the missing sector might be your neighbor's living room. In that case, you will need to work from within your own living space.

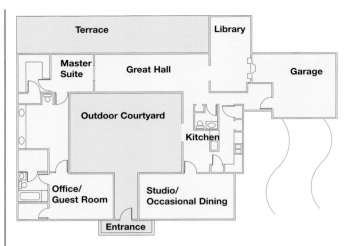

Plan A. This floor plan features an inner courtyard with a pond. This inner room is open to the elements and provides an intimate connection between the inhabitants and earth energy. However, a few adjustments are necessary to make this house harmonious with the ba gua.

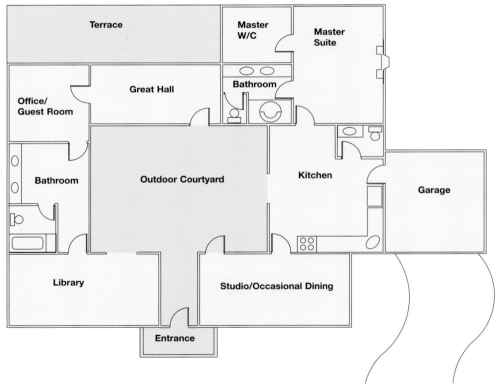

In the original floor plan, the library is positioned in the Intimate Relationships area and the bedroom is in Abundance. This adjusted floor plan has moved the bedroom to the Intimate Relationships area, the library into Self-knowledge, and the office into Abundance. Now the purpose and function of each room matches the energy of its location.

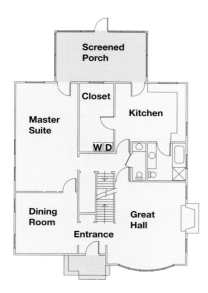

Plan B. The above floor plan opens onto a staircase, which creates a volatile fast-moving chi that flows right out the front door.

The adjusted floor plan (below) turns the staircase to prevent chi from draining and creates a spacious entry area. It reduces the size of the porch to avoid creating a missing area in the back. The location of the master bedroom and kitchen have been traded to match the ba gua sectors.

Plan C. The above floor plan is dominated by the garage. To reduce this prominence and balance energy throughout the home, the floor plan below makes several adjustments.

The entrance into the garage is turned to the side and a window is placed to face the front, making the garage look like living space. The home office and laundry areas are pushed out to fill in the outline of the house and bring more chi into the Journey and Self-knowledge areas. The bedroom and family areas are extended to eliminate missing Abundance and Fame areas. The master suite enhances energy in Intimate Relationships.

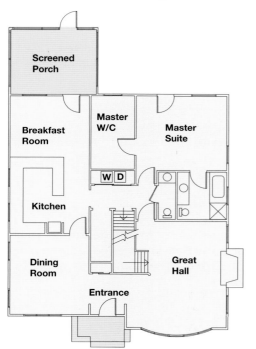

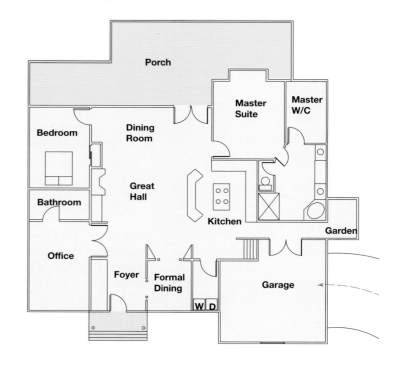

Organize each room by enhancing each gua with appropriate furniture and furnishings to balance and complement the room.

How does the ba gua apply to an individual room?

The ba gua is a metaphor (template) for understanding how energy flows. You can apply this template to an individual room, as well as to the entire house. As with the house, you determine the layout of the ba gua by the door into the room. If a room has more than one door, and if you use them equally, the door that lines up with the front door should be used.

The door into the room will line up with one of the bottom three sectors: Self-knowledge on the left, Journey in the middle, and Helpful People on the right. These are the three entry sectors. The other sectors always have the same positions relative to the entry sectors.

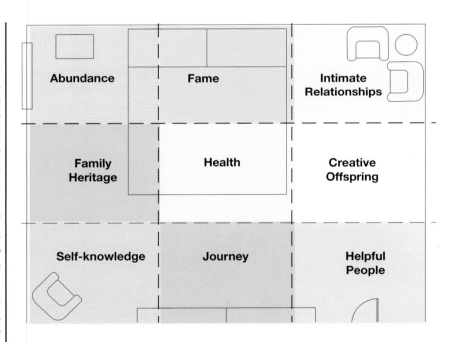

Chi flows into the Helpful People sector in this bedroom. Your bedroom door will either fall in the Self-knowledge, Journey, or Helpful People sectors of the room. The same rules apply to extensions and missing sectors.

Ba gua room-by-room

Journey (career)

Entrance. A Journey sector in your entrance affords you numerous opportunities to infuse new energy into your career. To announce to yourself and the universe that you are willing to show up and give your gifts, turn the porch lights on every evening, open the door to let fresh air in, and make certain the doorbell functions properly.

To stop backbiting or gossiping, hang gourds or bamboo on your door. The hollowed out spaces in the gourds and the bamboo trap negative energy and open up enough psychic space to allow you to respond rather than react when work gets challenging.

Bathroom. Although it is not common, it is possible to end up with a bathroom in your Journey sector. The water energy of the bathroom will work to enhance your career, keeping things moving and energy flowing there, as long as the energy that drains away is replenished.

Certain items hold symbolic significance. For instance, frogs are associated with abundance and prosperity.

If you want to change jobs, guide new opportunities to your door by displaying colorful flowers along the walk.

The wave pattern in the tile enhances the water element that governs the Journey sector.

Fix a round faceted crystal to the base of a hanging light fixture to refract the light and balance the chi.

Hallway/stairs. Stairs in Journey often find their way to the front door, funneling chi out of the house and away from those that live there. With a front door located in Journey, you might find that your job drains much of your life's energy. To slow and disperse the chi, place a large earthen pot with a live healthy plant in it at the base the stairs or at the side of the door.

Living room. A living room in Journey is great if you entertain as part of your job or if you are involved in a social occupation where you interact with people all day long. Think about the aspects of your job that you enjoy the most and represent them in your space. If you like writing, hang an intricate weaving on the wall to represent the process of bringing your ideas together in a balanced, creative way. If you enjoy a steady consistent income you can include a tortoise, the traditional symbol of longevity and consistency in career.

Kitchen. Not applicable.

If you love to be with people and have a career that requires some social savvy, add an entertaining piece such as a backlit liquor cabinet, a piano, or a sound system.

Dining room. The quality of the meals you eat reflects your relationship with work. If you tend to rush through meals, you will have the same tendency at work.

Storage area. If you feel like you have been put on perpetual hold, you can shift that by making a few changes in your storage area. Add a higher wattage bulb. Organize and prune it. Look at what you are storing in there. If what you are storing is mundane, do not expect your job to present exciting new challenges. To activate your career energy, place a mirror at the back of the closet or storage room directed towards the door.

If you honor yourself with healthy, balanced meals, you are more likely to find a healthy balance between home and work life.

Many career plans have been made and ideas hatched over dinner, so do not underestimate the power of a dining room in Journey. Whoever sits in the power position at the table (back to a solid wall with a view of all the doors) will enjoy greater power and esteem in the workplace.

To feel supported in your career, make certain you have a solid headboard behind you. The tall footboard in this room provides shelter from the chi of the door.

To attract a new job, place a spotlight on the outside of the garage door or leading up to the garage, illuminating your passage into a new career.

Bedroom. Bedrooms resonate with Journey energy. As a place of rest and rejuvenation, the bed prepares the way for a new beginning every day. If you feel constricted in your bedroom and have to maneuver around furniture, you will carry this constriction in your body each day as you go to work. If you have lots of open space in your bedroom, chances are that you will feel expansive when you get to work and draw new opportunities your way.

Garage. A garage is transitory, focused on coming and going. This instability in your Journey area can mean lots of starts and stops. To balance this, draw the garage into the living space by placing objects on the walls and by the door that one would normally expect to find inside. Children's drawings, potted plants, framed pictures, a TV or stereo—all extend your energy into the garage.

Self-knowledge

Entrance. The entrance through Self-knowledge encourages attention to an inner practice, something that strengthens inner resolve, peace, understanding, and wisdom.

Bathroom. Bathrooms in the Self-knowledge sector encourage one to turn inward and release what is no longer needed, including fears and perceived limitations. The act of bathing, itself, can be a meditation. Soak for ten minutes with bath salts to neutralize negativity in the body. Adding orange peels instead of salt aids the release of sorrow and emotional pain. A single orchid on the vanity invites stillness.

If your Self-knowledge area is in a hallway, place an item associated with inner wisdom somewhere in the hallway, and an associated item in your sanctuary. Visualize energy passing between the two items, linking the energy of Self-knowledge with your sanctuary.

A bathroom can be used as a sanctuary. If your bathroom is located in Self-knowledge, surround yourself with books and thought-provoking items.

168

Bring mountain energy into your kitchen by using granite, slate, baked-earth tiles, or other forms of rock and earth in flooring or countertop choices. Invest in the double-rounded finish for counters, so you are not slicing your aura every time you walk by.

For a Self-knowledge area in a kitchen, use stoneware pots to increase the association with earth and inner stability.

Hallway/stairs. The fast-moving energy of a hall and staircase is the opposite energy of Self-knowledge. Because this gua provides the grounding and stability for future growth, make certain all carpets are securely fastened down and banisters are secure.

Living room. With this combination, you have the most public room in the most private gua, a situation in which conflicts easily arise. You might feel too "available," as though your time belongs to everyone else. If you do, place a clock in the room next to your favorite seat to remind you that you, not someone else, decide how to spend your time.

Designate a favorite chair, one that soaks up your vibrations, so that it feels like coming home just to sit down in it. Indulge in a great set of earphones and turn stereo listening into a solitary pleasure. Discover the riches that await you inside.

Kitchen. Self-knowledge is the process of standing in your own strength, being your own mountain. Thick kitchen walls made of brick, straw, mud, or plaster not only give a room personality, they physically and psychically strengthen the person.

Dining room. Add a china cabinet to ground and stabilize the energy in the dining room. Because it is a heavy, stable piece of furniture, it holds a strong earth vibration. A china cabinet with an inside light represents inner illumination and wisdom. A buffet is another great way to add stabilizing earth energy.

If you have an inner practice, whether it is meditation, reading, yoga, or dancing, represent that practice on the door into your Self-knowledge area so you are physically reminded of it every time you enter the house.

If your dining room is large enough, consider placing an armchair with a lamp in a corner to extend the function of the space to relaxing as well as eating.

A single chair in the living room encourages solitude and reflection even if you never use it.

A beanbag encloses the aura and gives a secure, safe feeling. A dark-colored, cotton beanbag will help your children or friends release positive ions and stress better than light-colored vinyl.

Storage area. Store items here that instill a strong sense of self—a child's baseball mitt, a wedding gown, or a student ID card. A small closed space can be used as a sanctuary and assist in letting go of the external world.

Bedroom. The bedroom is a natural place to slow down and check in. Try using a reading chair or a bedside candle to encourage you to spend a few moments of mindfulness before crawling into bed. For children's bedrooms, use down comforters or lots of pillows to create a cocoon of safety.

Garage. Self-knowledge commonly ends up in the garage. Metaphorically, time for developing an inner practice is consumed with errands and driving long distances to day-care, school, or work.

If you like to read when you are alone, and Self-knowledge happens to be located in your garage, push some tools aside to make room for a few books.

Family Heritage

Entrance. Not applicable.

Bathroom. Downward-flowing energy is good for accessing past events and people. When we look down, our energy naturally moves into past time. To take advantage of this movement; add a photograph album of ancestors to the pile of books and magazines next to the toilet or place a photograph of your family tree on the wall.

Hallway/stairs. The hallway is a traditional place to display a coat of arms. If you do not have a coat of arms, display something sentimental. If you went on great camping trips in the mountains, hang a picture of your favorite mountain range. If you loved to sing together, convert a music stand into a hat rack, hang a trombone or trumpet on the wall, or frame a musical score. If you went golfing together, work a set of clubs into the decor.

A gallery of photographs or family treasures is a common way people remember their loved ones. The hallway and stairs area is the perfect place for such a display.

Consider meditating in the bathtub, especially if you want help or information concerning the past. In your decor, silver and nickel are the best choices for towel racks, lighting fixtures, and other accessories. Silver is associated with accessing past events and past lives.

172

Honor family members and ancestors by naming plants after them. As you nurture and care for the plants, you will find your family nurtures and supports you.

Living room. Parents are an important part of the Family Heritage gua. If you have unresolved issues with a parent, that issue will remain in your space in the form of stagnant chi and block growth and happiness in all areas of your life. Look for any large pieces of furniture that might block chi in the living room. Is your coffee table making it difficult to sit down or maneuver from one side of the room to another? Does your couch have its back to you when you walk in? Moving "block" furniture can open a way for resolving relationship issues.

Kitchen. Copper has long symbolized loving energy, so display your grandmother's copper molds. And if she passed on a sieve, sifter, or colander, displaying those will bring protection and comfort to your home. If you have a sharp corner that needs remedying in the kitchen, hang the sieve across from it. The holes in the sieve or colander can diffuse strong chi flows.

Invite your ancestors to be a part of your life by displaying their possessions. Share their stories with your friends and children.

Displaying family photographs and mementos in a storage area can create a get-away haven for reminiscing.

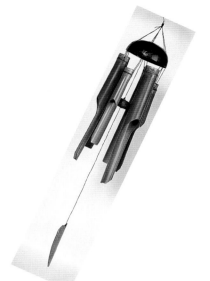

Bamboo lifts energy upward, creating a rising chi characteristic of the wood element.

Dining room. A dining room in Family Heritage is an energy vortex, a place where ancestors meet and interact with your present family. If you pull an empty chair up to the table, they might be coaxed to share their presence with you more often. For your table centerpiece, consider something with roots, stems, or branches in it. It could be dried branches from a nearby forest or wildflowers from your garden. When you look at the centerpiece, consider the many ways in which you are connected in this world and the prominent role family plays in forming who you are.

Storage area. Be conscious of what you are storing in this closet. Could you add your grandmother's wedding dress, photograph albums, your mother's dishes or bedding to it? If your entire Family Heritage sector is in a closet or storage area, there might be some family skeletons that need airing. If so, consider bringing your family energy out in other areas of the house. Look to see if there is a pattern with family energy in individual room ba guas. If you find that the Family Heritage sector shows up in a dormant or missing way in more than one section, use activators to get the chi flowing to that part of your life again. You can activate with lights, sound, movement (fans, fountains, wind chimes), or something alive (plants, pets).

Displaying loved ones' photographs connects families together, whether the subjects are living or deceased.

Ancestral heirlooms and collectibles in the bedroom create a bond between generations.

Displaying possessions from older family members keeps their presence with you when they are gone.

Bedroom. If you would like visitations from family members or ancestors in your dreams, include pictures of them in your bedroom. Add wood, plants, or upward-moving objects, such as bed posts, to support wood vibration in this gua.

Garage. This placement will keep your family origin and ancestors somewhat removed from your nuclear family because their energy is physically separate. Also, when Family Heritage is situated in the garage, you can anticipate more visits from or to family members. To ensure that the visits result in harmonious relationships, place a ba gua mirror (an eight-sided mirror that represents balance and harmony) in the Family Heritage area of the garage.

Abundance (wealth)

Entrance. Not applicable.

Bathroom. Abundance in the bathroom requires adjusting. Energy attaches itself to whatever has the most density, and the strong downward flow of water in a bathroom carries the energy down and away from the house. Prevent energy from the rest of the house from coming into the bathroom by hanging a ba gua (eight-sided) mirror on the outside of the bathroom door.

Hallway/stairs. Since hallways and stairs funnel chi through quickly, the natural result of this placement is money that goes out as quickly as it comes in. If the stairwell is not visible to guests, funnel energy up by painting an upward-moving arrow on the wall.

In the hallway, slow things down so that you have time to enjoy the benefits of your hard-earned income. Whatever is at the end of the hall should be absorbent, yin, dark, and sturdy.

This three-legged toad is associated with abundance. The ancient myth claims that on the eve of the full moon the three-legged toad would appear outside the home of someone about to receive news of good fortune. To draw good fortune to your home, place a three-legged toad in your Abundance sector.

In stairwells, it is helpful to place pictures or wall fixtures in a horizontal line to stabilize the downward-moving chi that is naturally created there. If you angle pictures down the stairs, it increases the downward tendency and can create chi that moves so quickly that it does not feel comfortable.

In the bathroom, remove anything that hangs down: plants, towels, and shower curtains. Add standing plants to move energy upward. (Jade plants represent abundance because their leaves are shaped like coins and move upward.)

Place the hand of Buddha in the living room to draw upon the energy of this tradition.

Living room. Since we tend to place our most opulent possessions in our living rooms, this placement works well for Abundance. The only problem is that people sometimes forget to spend time in their living rooms. If the room does not receive any active chi, it will stagnate and so will your cash flow. Make certain this room gets daily attention. If you are not into dusting or vacuuming, open the windows or turn on the stereo. Fill your living room with items that make you feel fully alive.

Kitchen. A kitchen can inspire a feeling of plenty. Stay away from stark black-and-white or stainless steel kitchens in this case. While they might feel clean, they will not promote Abundance.

If you do not cook much in your kitchen, you will need to keep chi active in other ways. You might want to add a ceiling fan (but not above the cook).

Decorative living-room storage cabinets in the Abundance area are perfect for displaying favorite treasures, as well as providing easy access storage for prized possessions.

Your health is an important Abundance attribute. Keep healthy foods on hand and continue to eat well.

Dining room. If you want more in your life than an abundance of food, watch carefully what you place in the center of the table. Fill a bowl with an abundance of flower blossoms, leaves, or fruit.

Storage area. If you want to hang on to and save your money, this can be a good place for your Abundance sector. But because this area of the house tends to be more yin than most other areas, it will have a slow chi flow. If raises are not coming your way as quickly as you would like, you might want to move things a bit, add a brighter wattage bulb or paint the inside purple.

Place an abundance of fruit in the basket or lots of potatoes in the bin to keep your Abundance area looking full and prosperous.

178

Nine I-ching coins in a box under your bed can initiate a positive shift in your finances.

Bedroom. There are numerous feng shui rituals that involve money in the bedroom. Most of these involve physically placing money within range of your auric field while you are sleeping. All these cures link your personal chi to the manifestation of physical money. When it is physically present, you will think about it more, send energy to that part of your life, and draw more energy in the form of money into your life. Be careful though. If your Abundance energy is directed solely towards making money, you might make a lot of money but not experience Abundance in other significant areas of your life.

Garage. When your garage is in Abundance, pay attention to your car. Your car is a reflection of you. Keep it clean and taken care of, then carry this feeling into your financial affairs. If you travel a lot for your job, consider placing a red envelope with a $100 bill somewhere in your car to show your desire for abundance in your career.

The pillars of this four-poster bed are great for a bedroom located in the Abundance area of the house.

Fame (external recognition)

Entrance. Not applicable.

Bathroom. Fame and recognition energy resonates with fire. Therefore, a bathroom in Fame is difficult because the downward-moving water energy of the bathroom conflicts with the upward, expansive energy of fire. Remedy this by incorporating upward- moving patterns. Tile borders that create a horizontal line halfway up the wall help hold the energy in the space and keep it from moving downward. Avoid hanging plants, especially over the toilet, and choose a shower curtain with vibrant colors and a design that moves the eye upward. Place a brightly colored rug outside the bathtub and be certain lighting fixtures direct light upwards.

Use bright colors and a variety of textures and patterns to keep Fame alive.

This bathroom is a strong expression of the owner's personality, which encourages her to be more fully herself whenever she enters the room.

A great way to bring drama to a room is to add crown moldings. This brings everyone's eyes up high, which raises their chi, enhances your reputation, and leaves everyone feeling better.

180

Hallway/stairs. Neither people nor energy spend much time in hallways and stairs. We tend to hurry through to another destination. Chi also hurries through, creating a volatile space where things can change fast. To stabilize, place a large object at the end of the hall, such as an earthen pot or a chair. Texturize the walls or use wallpaper with a lot of texture. Add a runner to the stairs or place a long thick rug in the hall.

To increase a fire vibration, make certain the hall and stairs are well lighted and that the ceiling is lighter than the walls. Avoid hanging light fixtures. Add bright colors in rugs, flowers, and pictures. If your hall is neutral in color, consider painting the door or wall at the end in a vibrant color. If you do not want to paint it red, go two shades lighter or deeper than the rest of the walls.

To provide a good view of the area behind you without cutting people up into pieces, use a convex mirror. The curve of the mirror provides a wide angle view of everything behind you without taking up a lot of space and becoming conspicuous.

If you have a fireplace in Fame, make certain it is never dormant. During summer months, fill the fireplace with flowers, lights, white birch logs, or something bright to bring energy to the space.

Living room. For a reputation boost, paint one wall red, the other three walls taupe, and the trim a high-gloss white.

Kitchen. The kitchen is a wonderful location for Fame. Your prime real estate here is the refrigerator door. Do not be shy displaying all the great things that everyone in the house is doing. Children's drawings, notices of school plays, flyers for workshops, newspaper clippings, or thank-you notes from friends. Copper is key in creating a Fame vibration in the kitchen. As the most radiant metal, copper activates dormant energies surrounding it.

Dining room. Whatever gets displayed in the middle of your dining room table should tell a story about you, your passions, what you love in life. If you love gardening, create an herb garden in the center of your table. Because Fame is the energy of transformation, butterflies, dragonflies, or a phoenix on the door are wonderful to display in this sector.

When choosing plants, consider palms and succulents. They bring in more solar power. Palms that fan out are symbolic of the radiant energy force of Fame and recognition.

Candles increase illumination and Fame energy in any room.

Storage area. It is hard to be dramatic about storage, but you can still influence energy. Use shelves to take advantage of vertical space and move energy upward in the room.

Bedroom. It is difficult to create a Fame atmosphere here. When we feel valued and recognized, we feel energized and passionately alive—not a state that is conducive to sleep. Find an area of the bedroom that is separate from where you sleep and dedicate that area to an awareness and appreciation of your own expansiveness.

Garage. If you can open up a window in your garage, adding natural light is an excellent way to enhance Fame energy. Make certain your overhead light is working and that storage is kept to a minimum. Get artistic in your garage—anything that actually goes through a transformation—on the walls.

To keep life's excitement use colorful, imaginative containers for storage.

Fame is associated with physical beauty. Find an area of your bedroom to dedicate to the things you find beautiful.

Intimate Relationships

Entrance. Not applicable.

Bathroom. A bathroom has a strong downward energy, correlating with a water vibration. If you tend to get emotional often, be aware that water controls the emotional body—too much water in Intimate Relationships can manifest in tears and depression.

If you live alone, make some room for another person. Buy a second toothbrush and pillow or include objects that represent the type of person you want to meet.

A bathroom is great for intimacy because flowing water deepens the emotional connection. If things get too emotional, however, stabilize the flow of water with earth elements.

Open staircases (above) in Intimate Relationships indicate volatile, quickly changing relationships. Stabilize open staircases by filling in risers and adding rugs, as in the photograph below.

Hallway/stairs. Stairs and hallways tend to speed up chi flow, ushering in change, movement, and shifts. If you want things to change, great. But if you want to stabilize the relationship, place a small convex mirror at the bottom of the stairs directing energy back up or hang a round, faceted crystal from the light fixture at the bottom to disperse the strong chi flow. If you have an alcove in the hallway, place a statue of two lovers there. (This can be as symbolic as you need it to be, depending on where your hallway is located.) If you like wallpaper, place a wide horizontal border halfway up the wall in the hallway to stabilize chi.

Living room. Be careful not to invite the public into your intimate space. This includes not sharing things about your intimate life with friends that they do not need to know. To draw the energy of intimacy into a more private space, such as your bedroom, link the areas by placing a rose quartz crystal in the living room and another one in the bedroom. Make certain that the one in the bedroom is larger.

If your Intimate Relationships area falls in the living room, use artwork to remind you of your relationship with your loved one.

Kitchen. The danger of having a kitchen in Intimate Relationships is that you will nurture and support yourself with food rather than with people. To avoid this, keep the people in your life physically present in the kitchen by displaying photographs on the refrigerator.

Food is intimate, so when you are in the kitchen, make it a time to talk about intimate topics. Copper has a long tradition of opening the heart, so use copper pots or display copper molds. To spice up a relationship, display your cooking spices, especially cinnamon and cayenne pepper. Stuff a pot holder with spices, add the spices to your cooking, simmer potpourri. The more you see, use, and smell them, the more yang chi will flow through your body and love life. To symbolize the union of your energies with your partner's, tie two dish rags or hand towels together and place them in the bottom of a kitchen drawer.

Dining room. A dining room in Intimate Relationships can help ground your relationship in the physical world. This area of the home relates to the lower chakras and will balance out an overly intellectual relationship. Because a dining room is a public room, have fun with covert expressions of passion.

Storage area. This placement signifies a dormant period in your relationship energy. Placing a large mirror on the inside of the storage room directed at the door can keep energy active. Even if it is your personal closet, make certain there is at least one item that represents your partner.

185

Keep Intimate Relationships in mind even in a busy kitchen by keeping a bottle of massage oil in with your cooking oils. (Make certain the children do not mix the two up when it is their turn to cook.)

Beware of placing packing boxes in the Intimate Relationships sector, as they may encourage your partner to think about moving on.

A bowl of pears in the kitchen or dining room can represent your pairing with your partner, without anyone being the wiser.

Uncut crystals in the bedroom are a constant reminder of mother earth and provide stability and support.

Bedroom. This is a powerful combination of energies. If you are ready to attract a new relationship, hang a man's suit (or if you are a man, hang a woman's dress) in your closet. Make certain the clothes fit your ideal partner's size and style. Get rid of anything that is filling in for a relationship right now, such as stacks of magazines or bedside romances. Take out the time-consuming computer and TV that tempts with 24-hour distractions.

Garage. The risk here is that you will see each other only in passing. Life is busy and you each have your own agendas, schedules, places to go, and things to do. To adjust for this tendency, place items in a prominent position that represent activities you love to do together. Avoid placing things in prominent view that only one of you enjoys, especially if it is a source of contention.

If you love to ski together, place your skis where you will see them every time you get out of your car and enter the house. If you love to travel together, place something on the garage wall that you found on your travels.

Creative Offspring

Entrance. Not applicable.

Bathroom. Metal gives its energy to water, so a bathroom here can drain energy from your creative storehouse. By adding earth you will strengthen your creativity. Add earth by using yellow or brown in your decor, bringing in terra-cotta planters, placing small stones along your window sill, or adding a bath pillow to your tub. With tile you can create a strong horizontal line around the bathtub, shower, or halfway up the wall. A horizontal line will strengthen the earth energy in the space.

Hallway/stairs. A picture gallery in the hallway does not have to consist of your creations as long as it inspires you to create. Use spotlights to energetically enhance your favorites. If you have a window, take advantage of it by placing flat leaded crystals in it or by hanging a radiometer to catch the light. The staircase can also display your creative gifts. Drape, twirl, or wrap tassels, lights, leaves, plastic fish, or whatever feels fun and playful to you.

187

Bring creativity into a hallway by painting a playful scene on a hallway door.

The leaf motif in the wall hangings and floor unite this hallway with the fall energy associated with Creative Offspring.

Set aside an area in the kitchen where crayons or chalk can be used for creative expression.

Living room. No matter how formal a space is, you can always add an element of fun and creativity. Find some way to represent your favorite creative outlet. Move beyond displays and show your playful side with furnishings. Remove the couch and throw a pile of oversized pillows on the floor. Place an antique door on a metal frame for a coffee table. Turn a walking stick or a trombone into a standing lamp. Paint a mural on your wall or around a doorway. Paint each of your four walls a different color. (This is much nicer to live with than it may sound.)

Kitchen. What better place to offer up your creative gifts—that is, unless you do not care for cooking. Regardless, choose a goblet to serve as your chalice and place it in full view to remind you that your creative gifts are many. With a white kitchen, throw a multicolored rug on the floor. Use all four burners on your stove, even if it is only to boil water. Use your refrigerator to display magnetized word art and play poet.

Make a formal living room more inviting and relaxing by displaying games and fun activities. Make an effort to actually play these games with family and guests.

Let a child fill his/her room with mementos and items representing things he/she enjoys doing. Photographs of friends and happy times are also appropriate.

Dining room. A lot more than eating can happen at a table. If you love to write letters, do it at the table. A well-crafted letter is itself an art form. Try out different tablecloths and see how they change the energy of the room. Although Creative Offspring is governed by the metal element, avoid metal/glass table combinations. Metal next to glass creates a precarious and volatile energy that is not helpful to human beings. Metal tables and chairs are rarely comfortable and are best used outdoors where the sun can warm and soften them.

Storage area. You may store something fun in storage, but be certain to bring your playthings out once in a while. If your creativity closet is full of boring things, hang something whimsical and playful from the ceiling. Write on your boxes in multicolored magic markers.

To add metal in the dining room, consider a metal light fixture, lanterns on the buffet, or metal drapery rods.

The metal base and the playful colors of the marbles make this fountain a great placement in a Creative Offspring sector.

Dreams are some of our best creations. Keep a dream journal next to your bed to help you remember them. Journaling unleashes the creative spirit and moves us through our creative blocks.

Bedroom. If Creative Offspring falls in a child's bedroom, set up play stations that are appropriate for the child's age. Choose toys that inspire creativity and can be torn down and rebuilt a hundred different ways. Make certain that this area gets fresh air often, at least twice a week.

Garage. Convert an area of the garage into a workshop. If gardening is your art, this is the place to display the tools of your trade. A garage also provides large walls perfect for painting a mural.

This hand-painted bedroom wall is a beautiful blend of creativity and playfulness.

Helpful People

Entrance. An entrance into Helpful People extends you beyond yourself, your relationship with a partner, and your family unit, into your community. Define the communities in which you want to actively participate and "call them" into your space. Calling in a community is much like creating a relationship with a spiritual guide. You place a physical object in the space to represent the entire community.

Bathroom. In bathrooms, we let go of what we no longer need and fill up with healing light. First make certain nothing is hanging over your head. No shelves or plants or even bathrobe hooks. If you have a window in the bathroom, a flat leaded crystal against the pane can bring in rainbow light. It will help balance your auric field and contribute to the healing rejuvenating vibration of the bathroom. Hanging a radiometer in the bathroom is also great for bringing in light energy to aid in healing. Work to include groupings of three or more.

Place three or more towels on your rack, three or more flowers in a vase, or three or more candles in the tub to promote community.

If you participate in a spiritual community of heavenly messengers and beings, surround yourself with angels to watch over you.

Bring music into the living room to enhance communal relations.

Hallway/stairs. The fast-moving energy of a hallway can bring a lot of change, fast, into your Helpful People sector. If things are moving too fast, slow it down with rugs, potted plants, or a heavy object. To enhance community interactions, think in groups. Place three or more candles on a table.

Living room. Since Helpful People is related to travel, it is a great place to display items that you brought back from your journeys. Those items hold the energy of the place where you bought them and they can call your energy there again. Use this sector to draw a trip to you. If you want to go to Africa, for example, place African masks or musical instruments in your living room.

Show your abundant travels in an exciting way, such as these tiles collected from around the world.

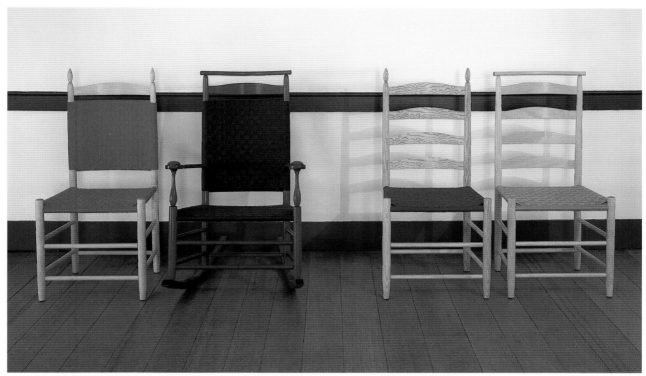

Mixing woods or styles in your dining set are additional ways to appreciate diverse energies. Use chairs from different time periods or paint each chair a different color.

Kitchen. Everyone loves to gather in a kitchen; give them a place to sit. Ring a bell or wind chime every day to welcome in helpful energies. Group spices or countertop items together to remind yourself that you are supported in your efforts. Make the refrigerator a community bulletin board and display notices of events that you would like to attend or support in spirit. If you have a garden and reap a fall harvest, dedicate a sharing basket.

Dining room. Embracing community is embracing diversity. You can create diversity around your dining table by placing a multicolored rug underneath it. Place a bowl full of fruit, leaves, or blossoms on the table. The round shape of the bowl represents the circle of community.

Storage area. This area could create stagnation in your social life. If you have not made new friends for a long time, or have not been able to "get out" and participate, activate this space by painting an angel on the wall or by stacking your boxes in groupings of three or more. Store items that you received from friends. Hang something circular such as copper spirals.

If you love travel, use a trunk as part of your living room furnishings and display your treasures from various trips.

Use the door from the garage to the house as a portal that readies you for a return to your inner sanctuary. Sanctify that place as a portal by painting the door jamb gold or white, and hang a small crystal from the top of the jamb.

The presence of angels in the bedroom invites protection from unseen beings.

Enhance your connection to other lifetimes and relationships by displaying silver elements in your bedroom.

Bedroom. Dreams and dream-time visitors can become an important component of your support system. The color and element silver symbolizes a connection to other realms and other lifetimes. You can add silver to your bedroom decor through a silver sheen in your paint color, silver items on your dresser, a strip of silver on a picture frame, or silver jewelry. If your bed is made of metal, expect to do more dream-state traveling.

Garage. Since it is related to travel, a garage can be a good placement for your Helpful People sector. Plaster travel posters on the walls or place an object in your car that relates to your next trip. The state of your car is directly related to the energetic state of your Helpful People sector. If the garage is clean and well organized, you can expect things to flow better. The right people tend to appear at the right time, connections are made naturally and easily, and you are aware of opportunities in which you could be helpful to another.

Health

Entrance. Not applicable.

Bathroom. A bathroom in the middle of your home requires adjusting. As water flows down the drain, vital chi flows away with it. Allow energy to flow back into the bathroom by placing large mirrors and upward sconce lighting above the sink. The lights move energy upward and the mirrors magnify the upward movement. Be certain mirrors are not hung so low that they reflect the water pouring out of the faucet. High mirrors lift your personal chi and expand the energy field around the top of the head. You should be able to see six inches above your head in any mirror.

Hallway/stairs. One of the most problematic placements is when Health is located in a hallway or staircase. When the Health sector is blocked with a hallway wall or an enclosed staircase, energies cannot flow from one side of the house to the other. This blocked energy pattern tends to repeat itself in the body. Place a picture in the room that has depth to it to create an energy passageway.

Carpet stairs and make certain railings are securely fastened. Place a round, faceted crystal at the top and the bottom. Open doors and windows to allow fresh air to pass through regularly.

Avoid mirrors with splits or two mirrors that meet in a corner. Both situations create a disturbing split image of the person looking in the mirror.

Place a large mirror in the room that shares a wall with the hall or stairs to create an energetic passageway between the hall or stairs and the room.

What you choose as a centerpiece represents the state of your health, so choose carefully. If you have flowers, make certain they stay fresh. If you have a bowl of fruit, make certain the fruit is ripe but not mushy.

Living room. This room typically works well because it has large open spaces. The most important feature of the Health sector is that it stays as open and free of clutter and furniture as possible. Avoid placing large pieces of furniture in the middle of the room and keep the amount of furniture to a minimum. Hang mirrors to increase the amount of space you can see from the living room. The more you extend your visual command of a space, the more you extend your energy. To further enhance Health, consider creating half-walls or opening up normal-sized doorways into larger passageways.

Kitchen. There are many varying traditions surrounding stoves in the Health sector. Some Chinese traditions view this as potentially harmful to the heart. Native American traditions view the stove as representative of all life force, and the central placement as being ideal. Our cultural associations affect how our bodies respond to this situation. In any situation, you can add earth elements to stabilize this area.

Use open wicker furniture to keep energy moving in a Health area.

If you have a choice, opt for an oval table instead of a square or rectangular one. Rounded edges will continue to move chi around the table and through the space, whereas square shapes will hold it still. If you have candles on your table, light them at least once a week.

Dining room. This open space works well for a Health sector. However, you usually have to place the table in the middle of the room. Adorn the table with a centerpiece which brings well-being.

Storage area. Since storage areas are typically small and closed in, this is not a good placement for your Health sector. Place a mirror on all four sides of the storage room or closet. This creates a vortex and allows energy to pass right through the closet. Invest in stacking solutions that allow you to create space in between layers of boxes. Place items on shelves instead of on the floor and keep things moving vertically as much as horizontally.

Keep your storage items organized and try to open up the space as much as possible.

Keep the bed off the floor, even if it is only a few inches and make certain you do not turn the space under the bed into an extra storage closet, as done above.

Bedroom. Watch out for that big heavy bed in the Health sector. Since the Health area requires open spaces to balance out and harmonize energies from all the other guas, a large bed can block the flow of energy and cause stagnation in the body. Keep under the bed free—chi needs to flow smoothly and freely under your body as well as above it for optimal health.

Garage. Not applicable.

Use lighter furniture to ensure chi can flow smoothly and freely around the room.

Where do I put it?

There is nothing more significant in feng shui than how something is arranged. The arrangement, as much as the individual items, determines how your environment affects you. Through arrangement alone you can slow chi down, speed it up, concentrate it in certain areas, or smooth it out in others.

Most feng shui is based on individual objectives, but there are a few things that are best to avoid no matter your objectives. It is important to note that the dynamics created by certain furniture placements are not "bad" in the typical meaning of that word. Energy currents that energize and stimulate a cat will kill a bird, and some chi flows are too intense or too fast to be helpful to the human body. The suggestions in this chapter will help you avoid placements that may undermine the immune system or disturb the psyche.

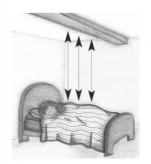

When you sleep under a beam, your body is exposed to the beam's intense energy when it is trying to relax.

Ceiling beams

A beam protruding out of a ceiling disrupts the flow of energy across the ceiling. Because beams are made from dense materials, typically wood or metal posts, they pull energy from the surrounding area and send it downward. You may experience an overall drain on the immune system, since the time your body normally spends relaxing and rebuilding is spent combatting the beam. Even if you have to move your bed or couch to a less than opportune place, keep it out from under the beam.

The energy from these ceiling beams interacts with the bed's occupant throughout the night. Covering the beams or a canopy bed may alleviate the pressure of the energy.

The painted waves on this beam visually lift your energy.

If bamboo flutes do not match the decor of your home or your symbolic system, try these:

▲ Paint the beam the same color as the ceiling to wrap energy around the beam instead of sending it down.

▲ Trail a living plant such as ivy along the beam to soften chi flow.

▲ Paint something (vines, coat of arms, flowers, or angels) on the beam to visually lift energy. This will train your body to respond differently to the presence of the beam.

▲ Use angels positioned at 45-degree angles on the beam sides. Energy moves in a default pattern unless acted upon by your intent. Intent alone can soften and disperse energy from the beam. Angels are strong reminders of that intent.

▲ If the beam is in your bedroom, move energy upward with a four-poster bed.

▲ Drape netting, gauze, or a swag over your bed. This literally carries energy across the top and sends it cascading down the sides where it will not harm you.

▲ If the beam is in your living room, use a plant such as a palm tree and position it so that the leaves arch up and above the seating area.

What to do if you cannot avoid the beam. Since a beam causes a strong downward push, adjust for it by placing objects that either move the energy upwards or spread it out. The traditional Chinese adjustment for shifting the energy from a beam is to hang two bamboo flutes at 45-degree angles on the beam, lifting the downward-moving chi. Bamboo flutes have numerous cultural associations and can be powerful adjustments.

If your bed is under a beam, drape a cloth over the top, directing energy across the bed and down the side, away from the body.

Slanted, exposed & vaulted ceilings

Whenever you enter a room, you automatically extend your energy upward to find the ceiling. Once this relationship is established, you use it to stabilize your movements through the room. If the ceiling slants or if the beams are exposed, you constantly adjust your own auric field to remain "in relationship" with the ceiling.

Most homes do not have exposed ceilings, but many have slanted ones. While it is true that a slanted ceiling will elevate your chi, it can be quite disrupting, especially in bedrooms. You can do much with your furniture to balance the volatile energy flow that results from a slanted ceiling.

It is especially important to place something tall in the corners. Put pictures on this wall of anything that moves up, such as butterflies, balloons, planes, flying birds, or trees. If your pictures contain geometric shapes, make certain the shapes expand at the top. Live plants and lights on this side of the room will lift the energy and help the entire room feel more balanced.

On the wall with the highest ceiling, hang a tapestry or picture that directs energy down. You can tell which direction energy moves by following your eye movements. If your eye moves down when you look at a picture, then energy moves down. If your eye starts somewhere in the middle and then moves up when you look at it, the picture is directing energy up. Positioning heavier furniture pieces on this side of the room will hold energy more stable.

Place items with a strong upward movement, such as lamps, tall chests, or upward-moving plants, on the wall with the lowest ceiling.

The low, cushioned couches create much needed stability for a room with a vaulted ceiling.

Windows

Windows let in vital natural sunlight, but depending on the time of day and your needs, you might not want to sit in front of them. A general rule of feng shui is to protect your back, and windows provide less protection than a solid wall. However, during the day when light comes in the window, sitting with your back to the window will supply vital chi through the chakras on the top of your head and the back of your neck. In the evening, the chi flow reverses and a seat by the window will start to drain your chi.

▲ Use inset panes to break up large windows and keep chi from flowing out.

▲ Be certain to use coverings in the evening to keep chi in.

▲ Be aware of what you see through your window. The view is as important as the window itself.

If you must place a chair next to a window, make certain the windows have thick curtains that can be closed in the evening to minimize the chi drain.

Ceiling fans

A ceiling fan drastically affects your chi. As each blade cuts through your aura, your body sends energy out to restore its structure and balance. In the bedroom, when six to ten blades per second are slicing through your aura, it takes a lot of energy to keep reconstructing your field. As a result, you wake up feeling drained, bruises take longer to go away, colds seem to linger, and cuts heal slowly.

If you need a fan to cool things off, use a floor fan and direct the blades away from your body. Use fans in adjacent rooms, rather than turning them on in the room that you are currently in. In the bedroom, you can turn on your ceiling fan before you go to bed to cool things off and then turn it off while you are sleeping under it. However, even when they are not on, the blades affect you.

A round, faceted crystal can be added to your pullcord to disperse energy from a ceiling fan's blades and soften their constant effect on the body.

Chi experiment:
1. Stand under a flat ceiling and hold one arm down at your side, the other one straight out to the side.
2. Have someone push down on the extended arm while you resist. You should get a good idea of how strong you are by how much you are able to resist.
3. Now, turn the fan on and stand directly underneath it.
4. Have someone do exactly the same thing with your extended arm as before. (Your friend should not stand under the fan when doing this or his own strength will be diminished.) Notice how your physical strength decreases when under the fan.

Because this ceiling fan is not directly above the desk, it actually helps stabilize energy in the room by diverting the strong chi flowing down with the slanted ceiling.

Avoid placing breakable items, such as a glass table, under a chandelier to reduce its threatening impact.

Chandeliers

Any heavy object hanging over your head creates an oppressive and foreboding reaction in the body. Remember, in feng shui, the potential of danger can affect the psyche just as much as if something had actually occurred.

Exchanging a heavy light fixture for one that connotes buoyancy and lift like this one helps people feel safer seated around a glass table.

The uneven ceiling and sharp corner edges in this room create a volatile chi flow, making it difficult to feel balanced and safe. The competing attention of the large windows, the ceiling fan, and the pillars sends a feeling of confusion.

Sharp corners

When choosing between two possible placements, look around the room and see if there are any sharp angles (two walls coming together, the edge of a dresser or armoire, a plant stand, or floor-to-ceiling pillar) that point directly at you and where you will be sitting. This particular situation, referred to as "poison arrows," creates an intense flow of energy that is three to four times as strong as what comes off of a flat wall. This drains energy from the physical body because the body has to send energy out into your auric field to balance the pressure of the energy that is pointed at you. The more intense the angle, the more it disrupts your personal chi flow.

When you unconsciously position yourself at the end of a sharp point, it can reveal a tendency to place yourself at risk to smooth things out for others. It can also indicate counterintentions that undermine your goals.

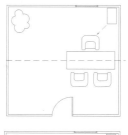

The placement of furniture in this home office drains chi from the person seated behind the desk because the filing cabinet angle creates a poison arrow.

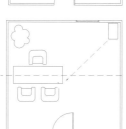

Simply moving the desk to the other side of the room shifts the angle of the filing cabinet and eliminates the draining effect of the poison arrow.

Priority placements

All you practical people reading feng shui books, this chapter is for you. The need for what I call "priority placement" feng shui shows up in those moments when you find yourself entertaining the thought of fresh-squeezed orange juice for breakfast, only to realize that the juicer is hidden in the back of your appliance cupboard. Too much effort. The urge recedes and you opt for the carton in the refrigerator. Had you placed the juicer in the front half of your cupboard, your experience might have been different. Another example of priority placement feng shui could find you unconsciously flipping on the TV when you get home, not because you want to watch what is on, but because it is the first thing you see when you walk through the door.

What is priority placement feng shui?

The priority placement approach recognizes that we humans typically expend as little time and energy as possible to get through the day. It is not likely that you will get the ladder out of the garage and use it to crawl up into the attic to get down the dishes for Sunday dinner. Items you need to use or places you need to attend to on a daily basis should be close by. The need for priority placement feng shui was made painfully obvious to me when I moved into my current house. I was dumbfounded when I discovered that, after 100 years of use, no one had installed a phone jack on the main living level. For the first week that I lived there, I ran up and down the stairs every time the phone rang, trying to remember whether I had left the phone on the charger. When I simply think of the combined energy expended by people running upstairs to answer the phone every day for the past 100 years, I am exhausted.

Make it easy on yourself. Before reorganizing, this formal living room arrangement blocked people from entering.

The new arrangement welcomes guests into the room and increases chi flow throughout.

Priority placement feng shui recognizes that we often opt for whatever action requires the least amount of effort.

—author

Without a piece of service furniture to act as a handy gathering place near the entrance, items tend to pile up. The right entrance container will have a place for mail, letter openers, keys, cell phones, sunglasses, and wallets.

Working with priority placement feng shui

Working with practical feng shui is easy and offers immediate results. It follows the cardinal feng shui rule that you should set up your house as a model of the type of life you want to live. If everything in your home is handy and you can get what you need with ease and comfort, your life will reflect this ease. You first must decide what your priority-one goals are; then you can place the objects necessary to meet your goals in a priority-one location in your home. This process brings your inner intentions into alignment with your external surroundings.

Priority-one goals

Priority-one goals are the things you would like to be doing every day. If you were to imagine your ideal day, what would it contain? Would you spend the morning curled up in a chair reading? Meditating by yourself? Walking your dog in the park? Chatting over a cup of coffee? If so, you should have a book handy, or a meditation spot, or a park nearby, or coffee on hand. What would you do in the afternoon or the evening? How much of your day would be spent alone and how much time would be spent with other people? After you decide what your ideal day would be like, you will be ready to set up your priority-one areas.

Priority-one areas

The places you go every day with little thought are your priority-one areas. These areas should house the most necessary items in the home. For example, the space between your parking spot and the door to your house is a priority-one area. Since you walk that 10–20 feet every day, put something there that needs your daily attention, such as a small vegetable garden. You could pull a ripe tomato or head of fresh lettuce every day after work as you walked into the house to fix dinner.

Over time, such placements will change the way you live. Set up your priority-one areas to represent and support your ideal life. Take a moment to think about what is located in the priority-one areas listed below and remove items from these

Items placed on lower shelves would be considered in priority-one zones since these items will be at eye level.

- Area between your parking spot and where you enter your home
- Area surrounding your bed
- Bathroom sink
- Inside of the shower
- Area within reach of the toilet
- Kitchen sink
- Front of eye-level kitchen cupboards
- Refrigerator
- Stove or microwave
- TV viewing spot (couch, chair, or favorite floor position)
- Passageway between the kitchen and the TV area
- Passageway between the bed and the bathroom
- Passageway from your home office to the bathroom
- Area within reach while you are seated at your desk

Priority-two goals

Priority-two goals are things you need or want to do every week, but that do not require daily attention. Do you want a clean house? Then you will need time and energy set aside for weekly cleaning. Do you want to socialize regularly with neighbors and friends? Then you will need areas set up for socializing. Think about your ideal week. Does it include one, two, three, or more non-working days? Do you spend full days alone, sharing your space with others only once or twice a week? Are children present part of the time, all of the time, or none of the time? As the designer of your life, what will you include in your ideal week?

Formal dining rooms are considered priority-two areas if they are not used on a daily basis.

Priority-two areas

Priority-two areas are places that are easy to get to, but you do not go there without consciously deciding to do so. For example, you would not open a cupboard unless you wanted something inside it, and you would not walk into the sunroom unless you wanted to be there. Place items in priority-two areas that require your attention on a regular, but not daily, basis. For example, you might go out on the back porch every other day to check the sprinklers or water the lawn. In this case, the back porch would be a priority-two area. If you have a reading room that you enter once or twice a week, that room is a priority-two area. Common priority-two areas are listed below.

- The back porch (or front porch if you typically enter through a rear or side door)
- The front of your closet (even though this area is in the front, the closed door means you do not see this area unless you choose to open the door)
- The formal living room or dining room (assuming you do not use these rooms every day)
- Craft rooms or guest rooms that you enter occasionally
- A den or office that is used weekly but not daily
- A garage or workspace that gets used often, but not every day

Priority-three goals

Priority-three goals are projects you have consciously put on hold or tasks that require minimal effort from you (like an automatic sprinkler system). Priority-three goals are also seasonal, and may move up to priority one or priority two at certain times of year (such as decorating the house for Christmas or deep cleaning in the spring). However, most of the time, they are of lesser importance. When considering your priority-three goals, ask yourself what you want or need to do every year that makes each season more meaningful.

Priority-three areas

Priority-three areas require some effort to get to. If you place items there that you should but do not want to attend to, such as bills that need to be paid, you are sabotaging yourself. Move your bills into a priority-one area and it will be much easier to pay them. Priority-three areas are fine for hobbies or tasks that are not pressing or difficult. As you read through the list to the right, ask yourself whether the items in these areas are things you would seldom use in your ideal life or whether they should be moved to a more active area. For example, if your baking goods are stuffed to the back of a closet (a priority-three area), but ideally you would like to bake bread every day, you need to change the placement of your baking goods to support your life goals. Or, if you want to start a business (a priority-one goal), but your office is in a dark and cluttered basement (a priority-three area), consider moving your office up into the living room while you get things going. Otherwise, you will need to transform the priority-three basement area into a priority-one or -two space.

- Flower or garden bed at rear of property
- An unattached garage or shed that is seldom used
- The backs of cupboards
- The tops of closets
- The cupboard underneath the sink
- Any cupboard or container that needs to be unlocked before it can be opened
- The basement
- The attic
- An off-site storage area
- A place on your property that requires more than a five-minute walk to reach

Priority placements encourage you to know yourself, to focus on your intentions, and to set up your home so that it supports those intentions. Now that you know where priority one, two, and three areas are located, you can evaluate your placements to see exactly what you have made into the most important things in your life.

Tracking chi flow through a room

Once you track the chi flow, avoiding certain placements becomes obvious. Placing furniture in the mouth of chi creates an uncomfortable situation.

1. **Locate primary door.** The main door is the mouth of chi and the primary source of energy. Chi will flow directly towards walls and windows. If there is a door or a window opposite the main door, most of your chi will flow directly through the room and out.

2. **Look for blocking furniture.** Check to see if your furniture blocks the flow of chi through the room.

3. **Rearrange furniture to be compatible with chi flow.** Use your furniture to draw chi further into the room, instead of blocking it. Move your furniture to the side of the main chi path.

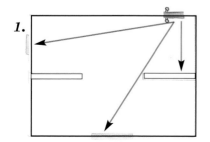
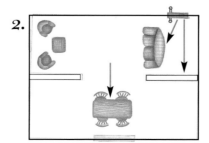
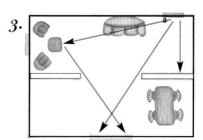

This closed floor plan blocks the flow of energy, and discourages unity and cooperation among the inhabitants.

Closed floor plan

A Victorian house epitomizes a closed floor plan. Victorians valued privacy and boundaries, therefore each passageway had an actual door. Because of all the doors, furniture placement became difficult. When rooms are completely separate, the inhabitants are left feeling separate from each other. They lose the flow of a harmonious whole.

Reclaiming floor space. Visually or physically remove doors without energetically blocking passageways. If at all possible, exchange doors that open in or out for doors that slide sideways.

One-way traffic. When traffic flows in two directions through a crowded space, energy gets jumbled and causes confusion. Determine an optimal path for the energy flow through your house. Then use furniture and picture placement to direct people to move in the desired path.

The wall down the middle. Many floor plans have a wall or hallway down the middle of the house. This divides the energy of the house into two separate patterns and influences communication patterns between family members. When you physically live in separate worlds, you are not inclined to communicate as openly and as intimately as you would otherwise.

In a room with lots of doors, consider placing a folding screen in front of an unused door to create a temporary wall. This will give you more options for placing furniture in the room.

To unite a room, choose a warm neutral color to spread light (and energy) equally throughout.

Energetically uniting the house

Color. When you have a closed floor plan, it is especially important to visually integrate your home. The easiest and most influential way to do this is to paint the entire interior of the house the same color or at least stay with the same color palette. Interestingly, Victorians traditionally used paint to even further separate the rooms of the house—the parlor was red while the dining room was green and the bedroom blue. Cool colors will cause spaces to draw apart from each other while warm colors will draw them closer together.

Decor. A common decor style and furniture period will energetically unite the house. Although it is possible, it is difficult to pull furniture from different periods together and increase chi flow at the same time. Each period has an energetic pattern that is generated by the shape, size, and style of the piece.

Lighting. Another way to encourage an even flow of chi through the space is to have the same amount of lighting in each room. When one room is considerably darker or lighter than another, they separate energetically.

An unused doorway, which was to the left of this couch, is now covered by useful shelves, which transformed this area from a walkway into a comfortable sitting room.

Open floor plan

Contemporary design typically considers the open floor plan to be ideal. The light and open spaces create a less restrictive closed-off floor plan. However, open floor plans have their own issues that need to be considered and adjusted.

Open is great, but this open floor plan brings an overwhelming flow of chi directly into the room. There is no opportunity to make the transition from the outside to a comfortable settling.

The room becomes more inviting by placing a screen between the entryway and the living room to create a transition area. The plant at the end of the screen softens the edge and moves chi upward. The added half-walls between the kitchen and the TV room, as well as between the living room and the breakfast nook, bring stability and peace into the rooms.

The addition of a screen allows for better placement of furniture and provides more privacy for the inhabitants.

To add stability in a room:

▲ Use large furniture pieces with padded arms.
▲ Hang pictures in a horizontal line.
▲ Use darker colors on floor than walls or ceiling.
▲ Use same carpeting on all levels of your house.
▲ Fill in open banisters or railings.
▲ Make certain all stairs have closed runners.
▲ Use large heavy objects at bottom of staircases.
▲ Place calming pictures at bottom of staircases.

The carpeted stairs and thick rug at the bottom of the stairs stabilize the fast, volatile chi of this open staircase.

The amoeba effect. Open floor plans make it difficult to create spaces that feel separate from the rest of the house. In this situation, you often feel as though no matter where you go, you cannot get away from everyone and everything else going on in the house. Consider replacing an open doorway with a door that can shut. You can also hang a drape to visually close off the space or use plants or folding screens to section off different areas. Choosing different colors and decor styles for different sections of the house will create a partial separation, but still leave things open and flowing.

Too much too fast. With open floor plans, energy speeds up considerably. If life starts feeling crazy and things are happening too quickly, slow things down by using large heavy pieces of furniture. Use textured walls, textured fabrics, and dark or muted colors. Carpet floors or use large, thick rugs (preferably rugs with simple patterns). Provide the ability to dim the lights and use window coverings that can block out the sunlight and chi if necessary.

Too many levels. Another example of an open floor plan is a multileveled house in which you are constantly moving up or down as you move through the house. This constant movement makes it very difficult for people to feel grounded in the house, especially children. This lack of grounding manifests in two primary ways. Either people will have a difficult time settling down, attending to details, and staying focused on a task; or they will try to ground themselves with piles of clutter, especially paper. If you find yourself pulled from one thing to another from the minute you wake up in the morning, chances are your house does not help you feel grounded. But, you can create grounding without opting for clutter.

Directing the flow of chi

If you could watch a sped-up movie of your family's movements throughout the day, you would have a good sense of how chi flows through your home. Interior doors, furniture, and floor coverings are key elements that guide us through each space, speed us up, and slow us down.

Interior doors that do not line up cause a distorted view of an interior room and cause an uneasiness in occupants.

Interior doors

Offset doors. Interior doors that do not line up are fine unless they are across a narrow hall from each other. Such doors create a distorted view. When entering or leaving one room, you see partially into the other, but not fully and completely. When your view is distorted, so is brain function. The traditional adjustment for this situation is to place a mirror or picture on the side of the door so that the mirror or picture lines up with the edge of the door opposite it. This will give the one eye more to look at than a blank wall and stabilize depth perception accordingly.

The straight shot. When doorways line up with each other, it is a straight shot. The straight shot allows chi to travel quickly and straight through a room. Sitting in the path of chi is not comfortable. The best adjustment for this situation is to place items such as a plant

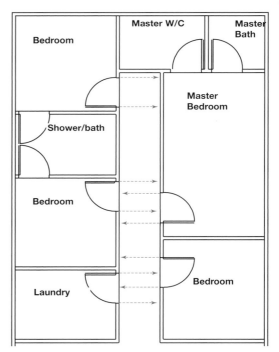

When doors in a narrow hallway do not line up evenly, you get a distorted view into one room when coming out of another. One eye sends your brain one message and the other eye sends a different message. This creates instability and confusion in the body.

To correct the straight shot, stagger items on alternating sides of the room or hallway to simulate a curving path. If you do not have room along the sides, use eye-catching pictures to draw chi sideways as people walk through the area. The low shelf in this photograph also helps keep chi from flowing out the windows.

or a folding screen on the sides of the chi path to coax the straight column of energy into a wave pattern.

Blocked doors. Doors that are physically blocked by stacks of boxes or furniture have a blocking effect in your psyche.

This chair placement blocks chi from flowing through the doorway. This translates into blocked opportunities for the inhabitants.

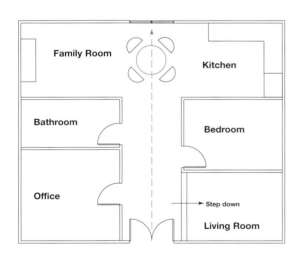

Be aware of what is in the path of chi. This straight shot from the front door travels right into the dining room table. This creates an uncomfortable feeling for those seated around the table.

Furniture placement

Facing your guests. More energy flows out from the front of the furniture than from the back. Therefore, when you turn a piece of furniture toward someone, you engage the chi of the person. This energetic relationship plays out in different ways. For example, it takes less energy to walk into the embrace of a seating arrangement than it does to walk around the back, even though it might take the same amount of steps.

This arrangement is open to the front door, but has its back to the kitchen. Although this may seem ideal when entertaining, guests assemble in the kitchen even if they are crammed, because they feel segregated in the living room.

When the furniture arrangement was changed so the chi flowed naturally from the kitchen, through the dining room, and into the living room, guests flowed from room to room, allowing chi to flow as well.

Floor coverings. Certain floor coverings are more yang and speed up chi flow, others are more yin and slow things down. When you incorporate yin flooring choices, such as rugs and carpets, you encourage people to sit down and relax. Hardwood floors and tile work well for walkways and areas where you want people to keep moving. An entire room of hardwood or tile flooring with no rugs leaves people looking for a place to rest. Use rugs under your conversation areas to provide grounding and to slow the chi for people to feel comfortable. In addition to anchoring conversation areas, rugs are key elements in directing traffic flow.

Although you do not consciously look down, you automatically move in whatever direction the rug is angled. In these photographs, the first rug placement leads people right into the mirror wall, the second placement guides them into the next room. If you want people to enter one room rather than another when they come into your house, angle the rug in the entryway to direct them. If you have one view that is better than another, angling the rug will automatically turn people toward the better view.

Furniture density. Furniture density is the proportion of furniture in a room to clear open space. Measure your walkways. If the pass-through areas between pieces of furniture are less than 36 inches wide, you have too much furniture in too small of a space. If your furniture is too close together, people will contract their energy more than they expand and not relax. Over time, your family and friends will be more stressed, more uptight, and more on edge than they would be otherwise. As a general rule, the furniture in a room should only take up ⅓ to ½ of the space.

The room above is overcrowded, making it harder for chi to flow. In the photograph below, the removal of a few items has made a considerable difference in the density factor of this room. The abundant quality still exists, yet the room is not overpowered by too many things.

Window corners have the opposite problem from wall corners. Instead of chi stagnating, it is funneled into the corner and out the window. Remedy this by planting trees and shrubs outside the window to slow the chi down as it leaves the house.

Corners. The two walls on either side of a corner push energy in and create a pressurized area where it is difficult for energy to move freely. It tends to get blocked and stuck. Some people instinctively place their furniture on an angle, trying to take care of this problem. If nothing is between the corner and the angled furniture, however, the blocked chi builds and pushes out on the seating area. People feel pushed out of their seats just as they would if there were too many pillows behind their back.

There is nothing wrong with angling furniture. A 45-degree angle imitates part of a ba gua shape, which promotes a balanced flow that is not too fast or too slow. However, this only works if you deal with your corners. Place a large standing plant or a lamp between the corner and the sofa.

To alleviate the pressure of a corner, place a corner piece such as this dish cupboard.

The curious effects of color

The colors in your home should support the way you live. This means getting the right balance between safety and stretch. Have you ever been in someone's home that you considered over-the-top, with colors so busy and intense you felt unable to relax? Likewise, I am certain you have been in homes that were too placid, unassuming, and lifeless in their color choices. You need to know your comfort range—the area between too safe on the one extreme and too intense on the other. Your comfort range is controlled by your personal need for a certain amount of safety and a certain amount of adventure in a healthy balance.

40% sepia brown

25% aqua

10% oatmeal

25% coral

How much safety do you need?

The evocative home follows the 60/30/10 design rule. This rule means that your wall surfaces make up the largest percentage of color in a space (generally 60 percent). The flooring, rugs, window treatments, and large furniture pieces make up 30 percent, and the remaining 10 percent is in the details. That means, if you select a safe wall color, you can use risk colors in your accent items, and/or in your window treatments, furniture coverings, rugs, and decor. If, however, you have a room in which you use a risk color on the wall, such as purple or red, you need to balance out this room with other rooms in the house, so that the house overall is not more than 40 percent at risk. The more of a risker you tend to be, the closer you will be to 40 percent in risk colors; the more conservative you are, the closer you will be to 10 percent.

The 60/30/10 rule:
Wall color = 60%
Flooring & furniture = 30%
Accent pieces = 10%

Most people need between 60 percent to 90 percent safe colors and 10 percent to 40 percent risk colors. This bright red entry door will increase the adventure for the San Francisco occupants.

The drama of black adds excitement to an otherwise safe color scheme.

Which colors are safe?

While color associations vary greatly from culture to culture (See **Color chart** on pages 242–245), certain colors and tones are universal symbols of safety. These associations come primarily from a color's physiological effects and its representation in the natural world. For example, the color blue will not make you feel safe in a kitchen. Why? Because blue food in nature is almost always poisonous to human beings. In this case, the same blue that feels comforting and peaceful in your bedroom can actually increase anxiety and discomfort in your kitchen.

This San Francisco town house has three levels and numerous angles, requiring a color combination of primarily safe colors. Each of the following items are "safe" colors:

■ dark taupe accent wall,
■ white surrounding walls,
■ dark green side table.

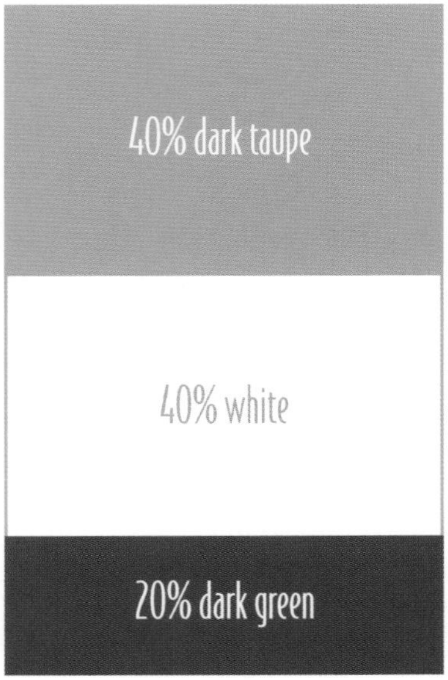

40% dark taupe

40% white

20% dark green

Reliable brown. Any brown tone—cream, beige, tan, taupe, ecru, ocher, toast, oatmeal, russet—is a safe color. Brown represents Earth energy—the enduring ground from which all nature's creations spring. Items made from brown materials tend to last over time, such as a hardwood floor or an earthen pot. Physiologically, brown carries energy lower in the body, helping a person feel more grounded and steady. Nothing creates safety and stability like brown.

Muted majesty. Adding black or brown to otherwise risky colors mutes and softens the tone. For example, red is normally a risk color. But if you add black or brown, you can produce brick red or maroon. Your body can relax and ground somewhat in a brick red or maroon room, whereas scarlet puts the body on alert. Muted colors create a stronger yin energy that will increase strength and stability in the home. Whether or not colors like terra-cotta (an orange-brown combination) or Gustavian blue (a gray-blue combination) are safety colors is often determined by the extent to which they are muted and the brightness of the surrounding colors.

Muted tones of any color help your body relax and become grounded.

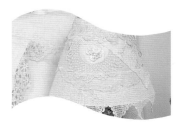

Green balances the metabolic activity of the body.

Fair white. White connotes perfect balance and fairness. White light appears white because it reflects a balanced distribution of all the spectrum colors. If white light was not perfectly balanced in its light distribution, it would appear dingy or off-colored. White represents fairness because none of the colors are left out. A note of caution, however. White provides a high contrast background for other colors, which means that it can actually make the risky colors even brighter or "more risky" than they would be against a muted background. Because of its high-contrast nature, white makes an area more yang if combined with bright colors. To soften the yang effect, use an "aged" white that has been mixed with a muted color to soften it.

Neutral green. Like white, green also connotes balance (in between cool and warm colors) and is the color that most often represents nature and healing (the Chinese view healing as a return to natural balance). Physiologically, green activates the body's metabolism, balancing catabolic with anabolic processes. In a home, clear, cool, or muddy greens are better on the wall, while yellow green is more appropriate as an accent color. Just as yellow green in nature represents something that is not yet ripe, yellow green in a home represents new and rapid growth and brings in more yang chi (change and risk) than blue green, emerald green, olive green, and sage do.

White represents fairness, being a perfect balance of all the colors in the light spectrum, visible when light passes through a prism.

Gold balances yellow's warmth with brown's stability.

Gracious gold. Although yellow is a risk color, a toned-down gold version with more brown than yellow is considered safe. Gold balances yellow's warmth and sparkle with brown's stability and comfort, creating one of the most emotionally and physiologically balanced colors in the color wheel. Add a bit of green, and you have a metabolic balancer as well. The yellow in gold activates the solar plexus, which energizes an individual's personal will or strength. Healers since Egyptian times have bathed the sick in gold light to strengthen their will to live and increase their ability to fight off disease. Gold is also the color most often seen by psychics the world over as the manifestation of universal energy (not the red of Chinese lore).

Which colors are risky?

Risky colors challenge you in some way. Yang in nature, these colors generate expansion, movement, or exploration. They invite you to open, to feel more alive, and to engage with your surroundings. They accomplish this by throwing you slightly off balance. They are the unexpected, the out-of-the-ordinary, and the uniquely personal.

Lively yellow. Yellow is the most visually active color. It bounces around a room, constantly drawing and moving the eye. By itself, yellow will tire the eye faster than any other color. Yellow also activates the solar plexus in the body (relating to a person's sense of personal power). This power does not always lead to harmonious interactions, however. Research indicates that babies cry and couples argue more in a yellow room. When you add yellow to other colors, such as yellow green, the effect is always dynamic and growth-oriented. These colors are meant to move you, not settle you down for a nice cozy nap.

Yellow bounces the eye and keeps a room active.

Provocative purple. Purple is a rare color in the natural world. In foods, it signifies disintegration and rot. In animals and humans, it is the color of bruising (also a sign of a hurt or damaged system). Because of its rare appearance, purple has become associated with royalty, since only people of royal blood could afford to have purple dyes used in their clothes. Purple is excellent for opening up the body's higher energy centers and for connecting you with the more spiritual part of your being. Still, you are better off not making purple the main color of your home, but using it as an accent. An entirely purple room can lead to mental illness and the disintegration of muscular tissue.

228

Purple is best used as an accent. In a dominantly purple color scheme, offset with white or gold.

Blue slows the metabolism and lowers the heart rate. Use blue in rooms where you want to relax and let go.

Serene blue. The color of the sea and sky, blue creates feelings of peaceful serenity. It is especially appropriate in bathrooms and bedrooms, but should be avoided in kitchens (See **Which colors are safe?** on page 224). Although blue is an appropriate wall color for smaller rooms, not more than 40 percent of the entire home should be done in cool colors (See **Your home's color balance** on pages 234–235). Too many cool colors in a house affect the body's metabolism and can lead to a weakened immune system.

Outrageous orange. You do not see unripe orange food in the natural world. Pumpkins, oranges, and squashes do not turn orange until they are fully ripe. Foods typically turn orange in the fall, just as the sun's rays turn orange in the evening sky. This time of day and time of year relate to the end of the work day (or work season) and the beginning of a relaxation/celebration phase. No surprise that researchers have found that orange rooms encourage less-inhibited behavior. The social nature of orange is evidenced in the body as well. Orange stimulates the sexual organs and other bodily systems that are more social in nature (such as digestion). Thus, orange is considered the most social color.

229

Orange is reserved for social rooms, since it excites conversation and lowers the inhibitions.

Red is a power color, but be certain to include it only in active rooms, as it activates blood flow to the body's large muscles. Red is often best used as an accent color.

Raging red. Fight or flight is red's evolutionary response. The sight of red, which in primitive times was often caused by the sight of blood, activates blood flow to large muscles so that they can spring into action. Red drains energy from the brain and encourages instinctive primitive responses, bringing the body's fight-or-flight mechanism into play. Bright red is also used by bugs, birds, and animals to warn off predators, since evolution has taught that a nasty sting, poison, or hidden weapon can be concealed by red. Avoid red-and-white combinations since red's complementary color is green. After looking at a red wall, the white wall takes on a greenish hue, causing nausea and headaches.

Note: Pink falls into the red category. Use it only in select rooms or as an accent. Not more than 20 percent of the house should ever be pink.

Reserved black. Black is an unusual risk color. Rather than opening and exciting a person too much, black creates withdrawal and introspection. Cool, aloof, detached, and reserved are all adjectives that indicate black's withdrawal mechanism. Because people are typically more withdrawn in formal situations, black has also become associated with formality, sophistication, and modernism (which represents detachment from tradition). This detachment gives black the ability to separate one energy pattern from another (such as a black picture frame defining where the picture ends and the wall begins). For these reasons, black should only be used to define a space, not fill it.

Black is formal, glamorous, and reserved. Be certain to balance a black wall with plenty of surrounding white or cream.

Safe color combinations

The following color combinations create a safe, secure environment, using a 90 percent safe to 10 percent risk ratio. Use safety combinations in rooms where you need to feel secure, comforted, and grounded.

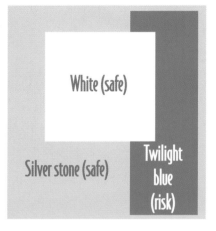

White (safe)

Silver stone (safe)

Twilight blue (risk)

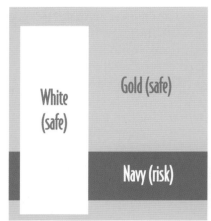

White (safe)

Gold (safe)

Navy (risk)

Golden haze (safe)

Deep gold (safe)

Pine green (risk)

Sage green (safe)

Creamy yellow (risk)

Shell pink (risk)

Tan (safe)

White (safe)

Blue (risk)

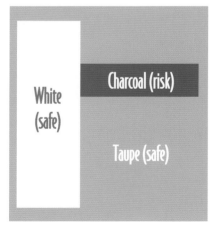

White (safe)

Charcoal (risk)

Taupe (safe)

Risk color combinations

The following color combinations invite exploration and adventure into the home with a 60 percent safe to 40 percent risk ratio. Use risk color combinations in rooms where you want to dream and imagine.

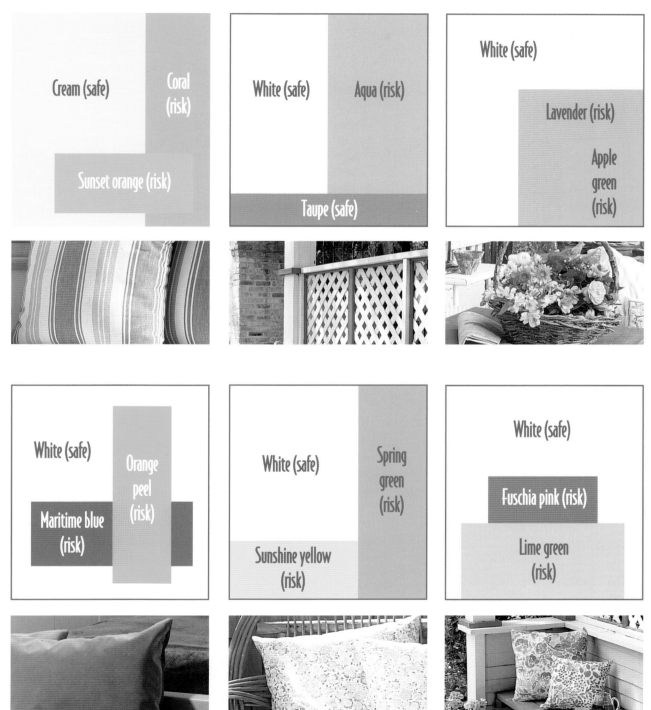

Your home's color balance

The human eye has a warm color bias. Humans need an overall balance of 60 percent to 75 percent warm colors, to 25 percent to 40 percent cool colors in indoor environments. Balancing cool and warm colors has more to do with the physical properties of the eye and how we perceive color than it does with personal preference. The human eye can distinguish four different colors through the cones: red, green, blue, and yellow (not the "three" primary colors you learned in school). The eye can also pick up a variance in luminosity (light to dark). With these six variables (four colors added to light and dark), humans see thousands of color variations.

The eye has adapted genetically. There is a much greater percentage of "warm color" cones in human eyes (cones that see red, yellow, and green) than the percentage of "cool color" cones (cones that see blue). This genetic fact results in strange psychological implications. If your home is decorated with too many cool colors, the cones will not fire as much as they would if you had more warm colors. When the cones do not fire, the light message does not get passed from the cones to the neurons. And what the neurons do not register cannot get transmitted to the brain. The result is similar to staying in a dimly lit interior and not going out in the sun. Over time, you are bound to feel fatigued, depressed, and run down.

Figuring your home's color balance. To figure out what percentage of your home has cool colors and what percentage is warm, use the 60/30/10 rule. If you have rooms that are not on the color balance chart at right, add a row for each additional room. Once you have determined where your home falls within the warm/cool color range, add or subtract as necessary to bring it within optimal range.

Using the chart. For wall color, mark the 60 percent row. For window treatments, flooring and furniture, mark the 30 percent row. For accent objects and decor pieces, mark the 10 percent row. Add the percentages for both warm and cool and divide by the number of rooms.

Color balance chart

	Warm %			Cool %		
	Walls 60%	Furniture & floor 30%	Accents 10%	Walls 60%	Furniture & floor 30%	Accents 10%
Living room						
Dining room						
Kitchen						
Great room						
Family room						
Bathroom 1						
Bathroom 2						
Entry						
Mud room						
Work space (office, den)						
Loft/play area						
Bedroom 1						
Bedroom 2						
Bedroom 3						
Closets (storage area)						
Hallways						
Subtotals in %						

	Sum of 2 columns		Total # of Rms		Home's Color %
Warm subtotal		÷		=	
Cool subtotal		÷		=	

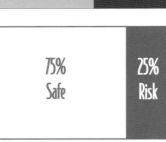

236 **Use your body as your guide.** So what percentage is optimal for you? Are you a 60/40 percent person or a 75/25 percent person? I suggest you use your body as your guide. If you are storing too much energy (bloating, extra weight, or emotional heaviness), increase the amount of warm colors in the home. If you are attracting more energy than you can handle (feeling flushed, hyper, anxious, or stressed), increase the amount of cool colors.

The gold and white safe colors on the walls are offset by the red and green.

Balancing with color

Paint can bring balance to your rooms in some fun ways. Varying colors and even shades of the same color can change your visual perception, allowing you to create some dynamic effects.

The long narrow room. Some living rooms or family rooms feel like a long narrow bowling hall. Paint color can help you here. If you paint the short end-walls one shade lighter than the long sidewalls, the short end-walls will seem larger. This is because light colors visually expand an area (make it more yang) and darker colors contract (make it more yin).

This room uses color to give more visual weight to the end-wall, reducing the emphasis on the long narrow side-walls.

The dark wall color helps contain the chi in this wall of windows.

The square boxy room. If your room is too boxy, painting one wall an accent color will shift the feel of the room to a rectangular shape. A brighter or darker color is best because the color will draw the eye and shift the focal point of the room to one end.

The wall of windows. A darker paint color can help you balance out a wall of windows. The natural light coming through your windows will instantly "fade" your wall color. The window wall will look washed out and paler than the remaining walls. Painting this wall one shade darker will help it match the rest of the room better and enable you to keep more chi force from going out the windows.

Naming color

I used to refer to "muted" tones as "muddy" tones, and then wondered why clients did not want to paint their house a "muddy" color. How you refer to the colors you select impacts your emotional body because the name of the color holds an emotional charge.

You can use this naming effect to your advantage by selecting a name for your wall color that embodies the characteristics and emotional energy you want the color to bring into the home. Consider the different impact of selecting "sharkskin gray" over "evening sky." They could both be a bluish gray color, but the name itself makes the one feel aggressive and masculine and the other feel peaceful and serene. (I will let you figure out which one is which.)

Set against a backdrop of neutral white, this mountain painting draws the eye away from the sharp edge of the wall.

The nine-drop ritual

The following ritual is a wonderful way to bring the energy of a certain color into a room without actually painting the entire room that color. If you are familiar with the colors associated with each area of the ba gua, you might wonder how all this color information is going to fit into those nine ba gua sectors. Do not worry, you do not have to paint your dining room purple just because it falls in the Abundance area of your home, and Intimate Relations areas do not need to be pink. The nine-drop ritual is a method of using intention to energetically charge your paint with the vibration of that ba gua sector's associated color.

Ba gua map

Abundance	Fame/ reputation	Intimate relations
Family/ ancestors	Health	Children/ creativity
Self knowledge	Journey/ career	Helpful people

Entrance

Purchase nine sampler tubes of paint, one for each area of the ba gua. (If you are using latex or acrylic paint, you can usually get samplers from the craft store, rather than having to buy pints from the paint store.) You will need: black, blue, green, purple, red, pink, yellow, white, and gray.

Perform the following with each ba gua area. Place nine drops of the color associated with that ba gua area (such as black for the Journey/career area) into each gallon of the paint you will be using in that part of the house. Using a stir stick, stir clockwise and repeat the following phrase, "I ask that the vibration of these nine drops energize and transform the vibration in this gallon of paint, so that the entire gallon will hold the energetic pattern represented by these drops. I ask that any natural forces present in my home who are willing to assist with this process do so now." Stir at least nine times, making certain the drops are completely mixed in.

You will not see a color change after performing this ritual, but you will feel a difference once the paint gets on the wall.

Making color flow

Second only to light, color carries energy through the home, linking one room to the next, affecting your emotions, balance, and overall mood. Just as important as the colors you select is the way in which you combine those colors into an overall house scheme.

240 **When every room is the same color.** The most common approach to handling color flow is to paint every room in the house the same color. This approach guarantees that the energy of one room will flow into the next and that the eye will not be greeted with harsh transitions as you move from place to place. This approach is fine as long as you select a safety color as your wall color and vary the 30/10 colors in each room. A house in which everything is cream-colored, including cream walls, cream carpet, and cream-colored furniture would be quite difficult to live in because it creates too much of the same energy pattern.

You can introduce a color into a room by simply adding a candle as an accent.

Honey-colored hardwood floors and rich wood accents warm the white walls throughout the home. The blue in this room sets it apart from neighboring areas.

By tying the color scheme into the brick wall and the green plants, the paint colors themselves feel more organic. The overall vibration of the home rises whenever you bring greater harmony to a combination of parts by drawing them together in a way that allows each part to share its energy with the other parts of the home.

The hallway picks up the terracotta accent color of the kitchen and living room as its primary color. The gold retreats and becomes the background color.

When each room is a different color. For "wild and crazy" artists, this approach seems ideal, and it can be equally wonderful. Balance is the key to making it work. What feels balanced to you will depend on how much safety and how much risk you need.

Decide on three to four colors. For your color theme, these colors need to play well together. Use both safety and risk colors in your combination to make certain it will serve your energetic and   physical body, as well as your design sense. Three-color schemes are suitable for smaller homes. Once you move into more than four rooms, you will need four colors to create enough variety in your combinations. (See **Safe color combinations** on page 234 and **Risk color combinations** on page 233 for help selecting balanced color schemes.)

241

Plug the colors in your scheme into different parts of the 60/30/10 rule. Use this method in different rooms. By changing the percentage of each color in various rooms, you can achieve variety while maintaining flow throughout the home overall. For example, you might use burgundy on your living-room walls, on the tablecloth in the dining room, and on the rug in your hallway.

Select a unifying color that will show up in every room in the same way. For example, visually unite your rooms by painting the trim white in each room, using hardwood floors in each room, or selecting chrome fixtures in each room.

The gold walls are the primary color in this room. The green couch and plants are supporting accents.

Color chart

Color is more than the sum of its meanings. That said, the chart below (each color's qualities are listed in order of lowest to highest consciousness) can help you scan for colors whose meanings will suit and support the intended energy of a specific room or project.

	Physical effects	Cultural associations	Emotional impact	Psychological attributes
Red				
	Increases heart rate, increases blood pressure and blood flow, increases adrenaline, drains blood from the brain and redirects it to large muscle groups (acting without thinking)	**China:** Energy, good luck **USA:** Courage, passion **India:** Marriage **Native American:** Faith, communication **Universal:** Nature's sex stimulus, as in red lips	Angry, outraged, irritable, passionate, courageous 	**Red:** Domination, survival, confrontation, aggression, self-absorption, good luck, audacity, activity, courage **Maroon:** Self-sacrifice (combines red's courage with black's association with death) **Magenta:** Innovation (combines red's audacity with purple's insightfulness)
Pink				
	Balances the effects of red with those of white 	**USA:** Physical weakness **China:** Marriage **Native American:** Creativity, working **Universal:** Romantic love	Weepy, needy, friendly, tender, compassionate 	Instability, immaturity, femininity, softness, sensitivity, faithfulness, self-love
Orange				
	Balances the hormones; stimulates sexual organs; aids with infertility; governs the intestines, lower abdominals, adrenals, and kidneys; helps body recover from shock	**USA:** Clowns and false attempts at cheerfulness, obesity **Tibet:** Eternal life **Native American:** Kinship, learning **Universal:** Fruit and fruitfulness	Desirous, encouraging, cheerful, happy, concerned for others' well-being, content	Deceit, overpowering, hyperactivity, stimulation, attraction, success, playfulness, sociability, joy

	Physical effects	Cultural associations	Emotional impact	Psychological attributes
Yellow	Stimulates the liver, pancreas, solar plexus, spleen, and middle stomach; affects the nervous system; stimulates the flow of gastric juices (which helps release fears, phobias, and physical toxins); stimulates lymphatic system (which relieves menstrual difficulties)	**Tibetan:** Buddhist monk robes **Pagan cultures:** Sun worship **Europe:** Lower classes **USA:** Federal yellow, colonial times **Native American:** Love, overcoming challenges **Universal:** Sunshine, energy source, commonality	Mean, anxious, sassy, egocentric, optimistic, confident, cheerful, happy 	**Yellow:** Treachery, manipulation, craftiness, verbal expression, charm, mental acuteness, accelerated memory, confidence, strength, intelligence, personal power **Green-yellow:** Cowardice **Gold:** Affluence, persuasion, attraction of cosmic influences
Green	Activates the body's metabolism, balancing catabolic with anabolic processes 	**Egyptian myths:** Osiris, god of death; ironically meant hope/spring **Celtic myths:** Green man, god of fertility **Greek myths:** Olive green, the symbol for peace **Roman myths:** Venus, goddess of love attracted to emerald green **Middle ages:** Fertility symbol **USA:** Money, finances, employment **Native American:** Living willfully **Asian:** Prosperity, luck, eternity **Universal:** Nature, growth, health, freshness	Betrayed, envious, jealous, greedy, trapped, ambitious, united with someone or a cause, loving	**Green:** Indecisive, easygoing, family focus, longevity, health, balance, harmony **Dark green:** Ambition, greed, financial prosperity, long-term success 

	Physical effects	Cultural associations	Emotional impact	Psychological attributes

Blue

Physical effects	Cultural associations	Emotional impact	Psychological attributes
Affects the throat, thyroid gland, and the base of the skull; slows the respiratory system; lowers blood pressure; stabilizes erratic heart rate **Indigo blue:** Affects sinus glands, eyes, and pineal gland	**Roman empire:** Public servant uniforms **USA:** Police and other public servants, solitude **Native American:** Intuition **Universal:** Loyalty, honesty	Depressed, withdrawn, lonely, sad, peaceful, understanding, tranquil, forgiving 	Depression, sadness, truthfulness, loyalty, wisdom **Light blue:** Patience **Dark blue:** Impulsivity 

Purple

Physical effects	Cultural associations	Emotional impact	Psychological attributes
Stimulates the top of the head including brain activity, scalp, crown, and pineal gland	**Europe:** Royalty **USA:** Luxury, gay (lavender) **Native American:** Wisdom, gratitude, spiritual healing **Universal:** Nature's symbol for poison, rarity, spiritual	Suicidal, depressed, calm, in tune, ethereal, enlightened 	**Purple:** Obsession, tension, ambition, progression, psychic ability, power, spirituality, wisdom **Lavender:** Mental illness, intuition, dignity

White

Physical effects	Cultural associations	Emotional impact	Psychological attributes
Absorbs none of the color rays, bouncing all the colors back to the eye; cleanses imbalances from the entire body	**Asian:** Mourning (they wear white to funerals to keep spirits from invading their auras), children **USA:** Sterile, neutral **Native American:** Magnetism, sharing **Universal:** Purity, cleanliness, innocence, balance,	Cold, distant, disconnected, sarcastic, peaceful, sincere 	Sterility, sarcasm, sharpness, balance, inclusivity, fairness, exactness, precision, spirituality

244

Physical effects	Cultural associations	Emotional impact	Psychological attributes
Black			
Black absorbs all the color rays, reflecting nothing back to the eye; slows all bodily processes (which can help with hyperactivity); draws energy inward; promotes retention of fluids	**Europe:** Black priest robes signify submission to God **Native American:** Hearing from within, harmony, listening **Asian:** Water energy, feminine energy **USA:** Formal, modernism, the unconscious, protection **Universal:** Formality, death, absorption	Suicidal, depressed, negative, heavy, confused, insecure, vengeful, protected, safe, still, serene 	Evil, villainous, draining, discord, submission, modern, formal, sophisticated, prudent, authoritative, powerful 
Gray			
Considered the result of a physiological breakdown or disintegration of bodily tissue	**Asian:** Community, travel, spirit entities **Native American:** Honor, friendship **Universal:** Spoiled food	Apathetic, passive, uncommunicative, neutral, calm	**Gray:** Collapse, disease, decay, confusion, self-reliance, self-sufficiency, mediation, complexity, neutrality **Silver:** Dreaming, astral connection, stability
Brown			
Brings energy into the lower half of the body, slows metabolism, increases catabolic activity (which builds up muscles, tissues, and other growths)	**Japan:** Neutrality, connection with nature **USA:** Material increase, telepathy, associated with animals **Native American:** Knowing, self-discipline **Universal:** Solid, stable, mature, earthy	Indecisive, hesitant, stuck, comfortable, grounded, calm 	Barren, restrictive, masculinity, being comfortable, studiousness, reliability, genuineness 

This magical place evokes the energies of many shapes, bringing them all into perfect balance. The branching triangle of the bougainvillea, the pillar in the upward-rising fireplace, the rectangular tile inset, and the curved arch in the twig chair all rest on a grounded foundation of brick squares.

I believe that good design is magical and not to be lightly tinkered with. The difference between a great design and a lousy one is in the meshing of the thousand details.
—Ted Nelson

Feng shui shapes

The shape of an object directs every energy force that interacts with it. How shapes move energy has been studied for thousands of years, with Egyptian, Hebrew, Greek, Roman, Native American, and Hindu cultures all contributing their puzzle piece. This study forms the center of our space program and allows airplanes to fly and aerodynamic cars to drive faster. Even in your living room—cupping a round wooden bowl or flattening your hand along the top of a table—shape alters your experience.

The center and the edge

Every shape must have a center, a pivot point. In feng shui, the point is the place at which potential energy becomes manifest in form. From a single point, energy issues forth from the realm of the infinitely possible—pure potential—into the world of form and limitation. Hence, the creation of any object begins with movement from a beginning point outward until it reaches an edge. The edge is as important as the center. It is the edge that directs the energy of the object back toward the center, keeping the energy moving perpetually from center to edge and back to center. How the energy of an object moves from its center to its edge determines its impact on other objects.

A simple circle of grass can activate an otherwise dormant outdoor space. By defining a clear center, the circle also shapes the edge, pulling the furniture into an active and lively conversation area.

The three objects were placed on this table to bring the focusing energy of the triangle into the home's living area.

The year is a circle around the world.
—Dakota Tribe

Primary shapes

The triangle. Triangles are a means of moving energy quickly and focusing it toward a specific point. The chi gathers at the base and is directed out of the point at the top, much like narrowing the nozzle on your garden hose. The spray of water becomes considerably more intense and penetrating the more you narrow the stream. This means that the chi moving out of the top of a triangle is usually not harmonious or helpful for human beings, and they should avoid positioning themselves at the end of the point. Triangles should be used to direct chi to a desired location other than sitting or work areas. Triangles also represent merging heavenly forces with those of humankind and Mother Earth. Viewed historically as the three primary forces in the universe, triangles remind us to look at the spiritual (heaven), physical (earth), and mental (human) implications of any decision.

The square. Squares are nature's way of holding on to an energy pattern in order to slow change and stabilize a process. The four corners of the square form the foundational building block for most structures and even out the distribution of energy from the center equally on all four sides. All this steadiness is great; however, a house full of nothing but squares and rectangles might be too anchored and become rigid or inflexible. If family members tend to defend their positions staunchly, even when they have good reason to change their minds, you might want to exchange some of those squares for other shapes.

The sphere. Spheres represent wholeness, completion, and perfection. The entire energetic journey is captured in the sphere, from its beginning point to its fullest extension and its condensation back into a pinpoint at the center. Spherical elements remind the body of this constantly cycling energy pattern and encourage constant growth and evolution. Relating to community and helpful people, circles and spheres are about working together, rather than squaring off in separate corners. Anything round will keep chi moving, though, and nothing settles for long around a circular table or work space.

Kidney shapes. Irregular or kidney shapes are considered Water energy patterns, a representation of the Tao. They move energy out from the center in a slow, meandering current. The more curved the sides are, the longer it takes the chi to travel around the edges before coming back to center. To use kidney shapes in your home is to symbolize that you are in the flow and that all good things will come to you exactly when you need them.

The pillar. Reaching up into the sky, the pillar has the ability to extend your energy into places you have never been before. Related to Wood energy, pillars represent strength, perseverance, determination, and fortitude. Historically, pillars have been symbols of humans' ability to both connect and communicate with the divine. Temple pillars, poles, spires, even Jacob's ladder, are all vertical columns that direct the energy of the earth plane up into the heavens. Referred to as the *Axis Mundi*, this vertical vortex between heaven and earth was considered to be the source through which the heavens energized and supported the earth. Pillars also represent the human element in the heaven–earth–man triangle, because the human element stands upright on the earth and interfaces with heaven on the behalf of earth. The pillar is a strong way to help family members feel reconnected to something more than themselves and want to stand up and take action.

249

A pillar suggests a link between the yang energies of heaven and the yin forces of the earth.

This colorful stack of Shaker boxes creates its own *Axis Mundi* for this area, directing the chi straight up.

The arch. Ancient temples are filled with arches. The pillars of the temples rise up, supporting the arches because they symbolized the bridge to heaven. Arches today represent the influence of the divine on earth. Sunrises, sunsets, and rainbows all form an arch across the sky, bringing in heaven's yang chi in the morning and taking it away again at the end of the day. In China, the arch is related to the Metal element, the energy pattern of the Helpful People ba gua area. Use archways to symbolize a passageway to an out-of-the-ordinary place or connection with your own spiritual being.

250 This artful application of the sun's rising rays forms an arch over this otherwise square fireplace, pushing the chi upward and helping to lift the oppressive chi from the ceiling beams.

The cross. The cross represents the vertical pillar energy of heaven or spirit and its interface with the horizontal earthly realm. Stemming from Creation myths, like the following, the cross has been around long before its current association with Christianity. The Absolute "divided itself into heaven and earth, thereby creating the *Axis Mundi*—the pole situated at the center of the world, holding up the canopy of heaven and connecting it with the earth. It thus became the central axis connecting and penetrating the horizontal states of being by passing through their centers." (R. Guenon, *Symbolism of the Cross*)

This living-room arrangement creates a perfect cross, with the couch and chair on the horizontal axis and the ottoman and chair on the vertical axis.

Area solutions

The front door

Your front entrance greets society every day. More than any other entrance feature, the door conveys messages about who you are, what's important to you, and how you would like others to interact with you. As with every aspect of feng shui, the objective is to match the vibration of the entryway with the people living in the home. The more awareness you bring to choices such as "What color should I paint the front door?", the more you can transform your home into a reflection of your best and highest self.

The size, quality, and overall condition of your door reflects your social position and status. Money has a distinct energy pattern. That is why money attracts money and prestige attracts prestige. To shift the way the world interacts with you, you need to change the energy pattern of the entrance.

To activate energy in the entryway with natural light, add flat leaded panes or stained-glass windows.

To welcome abundance, be certain your front door is in good repair. Keep the door and frame clean and metal polished.

Draw the chi of money

If you have a single-width door, visually extend the door by placing chi activators on both sides of it. Use brightly colored flowers around the front door to extend the chi sideways.

Doorbells and door knockers connote the personality and social stature of the owner. The house number holds an energetic pattern that affects the entire house. To draw more prominence to the house, get larger numbers and use a material that reflects light, such as brass, bronze, or copper.

Even if you do not use your front door as your normal entrance, it is still the energetic face of your house, therefore the mouth of chi. To balance out energy flowing into your home from different doors, make certain the front door gets opened at least once a day and that fresh air and sunlight are allowed to pass through the door.

To balance energy in a room, place an activator such as this radiometer, a light catcher, a mobile, or plants.

Link the energy of abundance to your entrance by placing an object that represents abundance to you, such as these coins, in both the entryway and the actual Abundance sector of the house.

If the door indents and is hard to see, you can pull chi forward by placing the chi activators further out on the porch.

Choosing a front door color

You do not have to paint your door Chinese red for it to be good feng shui, but whatever color you choose will have an impact on the chi of the entire house. Because your front door represents the face you present to the external world, the color of the door will attract certain energies and avert others. Painting the front door is an inexpensive way to attract energy to your home to support your current life purpose. Consider changing the color of your front door at least once a year and make certain that it is sending the correct message to the world. Last year's color might not work to fulfill this year's dreams.

New growth colors inspire and stimulate change.

Stabilizing colors increase feelings of safety.

Relaxing colors mark a home as a peaceful retreat.

Activator colors get chi moving and bring something new into your life.

If you want the house to be welcoming, be certain house numbers are lit and visible from the street.

Lot size & features. If you have a large lot and your house tends to get lost on it, the door needs a lot of punch. Brown, black, or white is not going to work well for you. A house that sits prominently on the lot can benefit from more subtle colors.

If the lot slopes, avoid colors that create a water vibration such as black, cool blues, and blue-greens. A stabilizing earth influence such as browns, yellows, and terra-cotta are helpful for sloped lots. If the slope is extreme, choose a color with an intense wood or fire vibration that will shoot energy upward.

255

Because this house already dominates the lot, the subdued brown color helps restore balance.

256

Placing a windchime between the street and your front door will provide protection and safety.

To initiate a change in career, choose a door color that has the same energy as the career you want to move into:
▲ Counseling
▲ Sales
▲ Marketing
▲ Healing
▲ Service-oriented
▲ Entertainment
▲ Computers
▲ Design

Career needs. If your front door is in your Journey sector, make certain that the color you choose for the door is in harmony with your chosen career. If you have a high-profile career, you do not want a subtle front door. Drama and contrast will create the energetic push you need. Use more than one color on your door or add more lighting to make things zing. To calm stress in your chosen career, opt for muted colors in a more natural palette.

House color & materials. Your door should balance the energy of the rest of the house. If the house is bright and dramatic, the door should provide relief. If the house is neutral and subdued, the door should provide some excitement and the hint of the unexpected. Brick houses are already grounded and earthy and would benefit from a bright fire door. Wood houses support growth and upward movement and can be balanced by a water vibration.

If your house sits close to the street, create more privacy by choosing a subtle door color or by setting the door in a recessed alcove.

House guardians

Wind chimes have been used for centuries to protect homes and temples from spirits. Through sound, wind chimes warn of a shift in energy. Coconut and bamboo chimes work well as guardians because the hollow spaces represent psychic protection against the unknown. Metal chimes have the clearest sound, and balance energy in the body.

Dragons placed outside your home are an excellent protection symbol. Some dragons have a specific calling and blessing that they bestow on the house.

Frogs placed outside your home symbolize the arrival of prosperity and abundance.

Tortoises represent the steady development of a satisfying career that is built on compassion and consideration for your well-being and the well-being of others.

House guardian symbols of safety and protection can change as your needs change. Any winged guardian can protect you from assaults that affect your place in the community.

Whatever you choose to place in your entrance space sets the energy for the entire home.

The turtle as a house guardian symbolizes the steady increase of career chi and financial stability.

This glass door allows natural light into the home. The area rugs direct traffic into the main area of the house and away from a private office doorway. The two chairs to the side promote hospitality. The treasures in the curio cabinet personalize an otherwise austere setting.

Entry lighting

Lighting should be considered carefully. Natural light eases the transition, making it easier for your eyes and your energy to adjust to interior light. If it is not possible to allow natural light into the space, use full-spectrum lighting in the entry. It will also help if your entry is one of the lightest spaces in the house. You feel more comfortable when the shift from bright outdoor light to dim interior light is gradual rather than abrupt.

Inside the door

The entrance provides a place to transition from the outside world (a yang state) to your personal space (a yin state). If you walk through your front door straight into your living room, the transition feels abrupt and harsh. Consider building a half wall or create a divider with a folding screen, a wall of plants, or even a sofa table. This area should hold items that allow the transition from outside to inside to flow smoothly.

Track lighting is an easy way to increase overall illumination in an entry.

Placing shiny objects behind your burners allows you to keep involved with the rest of the room when your back is turned.

Display an abundance of spices and oils and use them regularly. If you need to have your knives on the counter, be certain they are safely ensconced in a wood block, rather than hanging from a magnetic strip.

The stove

The stove allows you to nurture yourself and provide for your physical needs. In many cultural traditions, the stove houses gods that watch out for your overall health and physical strength. Before stoves, the hearth or campfire represented the state of the family's physical well-being. As long as the fire was burning strong, the family's personal chi would also be strong.

When preparing food, you want to feel as comfortable and secure as possible. Whatever energy state you are in when you are cooking is passed directly into the food. Nothing absorbs negative emotions or stress more than food and water. If you are feeling out of sorts, grumpy, or stressed while preparing dinner, take a few seconds and run your hands under warm water. Running water can pull negativity and stress out of your body and release it down the drain. You will feel more relaxed and balanced, and the entire cooking/dining experience will improve.

The openings over the sink help those in the kitchen feel more involved with guests in the adjoining living room.

Stove placement & use

If you stand with your back to the room while preparing meals, it is hard to be visually and energetically a part of what is going on in the rest of the kitchen. If possible, position your stove so you are facing the room. This may require an island or an L-shaped counter. If you cannot face the room, try to provide a side view of the comings and goings. A traditional adjustment is to place a convex mirror on the wall behind the stove. This works great if you do not have a range top or hood above the stove. Another great fix is a shiny curved teapot.

Use all four burners. The stove is the central fire element in your house. If you only use the front burners, or none at all, you send yourself the message that you only want access to part of your energy reserves. Leaving a teapot full of water on the stove is another way to weaken this fire element, since water subdues the energy of fire. Move your teapot around to all four burners and empty the water out when you are done.

Keep it clean. Because your stove represents your physical health and well-being, keeping it clean reflects directly on your desire to care for your physical body. A clean stove keeps chi flowing smoothly and does not allow for stagnation.

An island in the kitchen, containing the stove, gives the cook the opportunity to be involved with guests in the rest of the room while cooking.

The rounded counter in this kitchen keeps chi flowing around the counter and connotes the auspicious ba gua shape.

Countertops

No matter what your countertops are made of, watch your edges. A flat edge can create a sharp arrow pointing right at you when you stand at the stove or sink. Use dowsing rods to measure the extent to which any sharp edges in your kitchen cut your chi. This is crucial if your countertops are made of granite or some other sharp material. Your desire to be in and cook in your kitchen will diminish greatly. To strengthen your chi and create an environment of support and physical nurturing, invest in double-rounded edges for all counter-tops. Although the single round is better than a flat edge, it still carries an undercurrent of sharpness.

Placing plants and upward items in the corner behind the sink will slow down chi leaving through the window.

The microwave placed next to this refrigerator creates conflicting chi.

Balancing fire & water

Sometimes the stove is next to the refrigerator or sink. These both carry a strong downward water vibration and are in conflict with the upward expansive energy of fire. To balance water and fire, place something wood between the stove and the water element. Wooden cabinets, cutting boards, even cooking utensils can all help create a balanced flow of energy instead of an abrupt transition. Also, be certain the microwave does not sit next to a water element.

The granite countertop balances the volatile chi of the sink placed next to the stovetop.

Things hanging overhead

Pots and pans. Think about the desirability of this situation. A bunch of large heavy unstable pots hanging over your head is not going to create an environment of safety, stability, and comfort. Just stand under your pot rack, turn your head up and look at all those pots. Do you really want the sensation of things hanging over your head?

If you need to keep the pot rack above your head, do not leave any of the hooks empty. Empty hooks represent a tendency to allow the moods and actions of others to trigger undesired responses. You are symbolically leaving yourself open to being caught by psychic traps, jabs, and pulls. Make certain that the hooks themselves are rounded, rather than sharp points.

This kitchen demonstrates a precarious situation, with pans hanging directly over the cook's head.

This kitchen provides a practical way to store and display pots and kitchen items without hanging them.

The matching lamps and nightstands represent equality in the relationship. The pillars to the side of the bed draw the blessings of heaven into this union.

The bed

Clear energies from previous relationships

Objects from previous relationships hold energy from that relationship, and can greatly undermine your efforts to do things differently in a new relationship. If at all possible, start a new relationship in a home that is new to both of you. There is nothing more unsettling than moving into someone's house. They might be saying "I love you, please move in," but their space says "Sorry, I'm already full of someone else's energy, habits, emotions, and tendencies."

If starting out somewhere new to both of you is impossible, making a few changes to the old home will bring harmony to the new relationship. It is crucial to start a new intimate relationship with a new mattress set. You are more vulnerable and intimate in bed than any other location, and the mattress holds the vibrations from whatever has transpired in that bed (especially a waterbed).

The bed frame, especially the headboard, represents how you and your partner support each other. If you want to do things differently in the new relationship, get a new headboard.

Even a nightlight can be symbolic. This one represents long life.

Surround yourself with sensuality

The most arousing thing to a man is a passionate woman. Therefore, women, do not feel selfish placing things that please you in your bedroom. If it puts you in touch with your sensual nature, he will appreciate it. Small additions like plush towels, new sheets, or erotic scents can have a big impact on how sensual you feel.

Choosing the right bed

Beds carry different vibrations. Shape, color, and materials influence ambiance. Choose a bed with the right energetic impact for you.

Bed shapes. Fire vibrations are not generally recommended for beds. Stay away from triangular-shaped headboards. Triangular shapes in your bedroom encourage triads in your relationship. The triad can manifest in the form of an affair. Also, do not place your bed on a diagonal, since that creates a triangle directly behind your head.

Flowers, oils, and candles have a long psychological association with romance that may or may not light your fire.

The combination of this water-element sleigh bed and the red fire comforter bring a balance of warmth and strength.

Earth vibration. A bed with an earth vibration will help you ground. It increases feelings of safety and support. Any bed with a solid wooden headboard creates an earth vibration. (Remember, the headboard represents your psychological support system.)

Bed textures & fabrics. Adding texture increases your awareness of your tactile sense, which puts you more in touch with your physical body. Soft textures in the bedroom encourage intimacy and the tendency to be kind to yourself and others. Cotton brings the natural world indoors and has a crisp clean energy. Silks and satins have a lush smoothness that allow energy to flow quickly. Chenille is nurturing and supportive. Use this to soften and comfort, but do not turn your bedroom into a therapist's couch.

Fabrics recommended for the bedroom:
▲ Cotton
▲ Silk
▲ Satin
▲ Chenille

A turtle filled with three I-ching coins under the bed may bring luck into a union.

Bed colors. Warm tones encourage physical intimacy. Although cool colors are helpful for inducing sleep, if your walls cast a gray or blue on your skin you will not be inclined to intimacy. It is best to use soft tones, such as a light rose or terra-cotta, that cast warm hues on your skin without being too physically stimulating.

Use peach carefully. Peach is a volatile color that initiates change in the body. Only use peach if your relationship is in need of a shift. Add peach pillows or something you can remove when you want things to stabilize.

Use black sparingly. Black represents boundaries and separation, and black-and-white color schemes create literal lines of separation. If you feel the need for strong boundaries in order to feel safe in your relationship, use black and white. If boundaries are not something you want to emphasize, avoid this combination.

Display photographs of family in your bedroom in silver frames to encourage dreams of others.

WOOD VIBRATION. Beds with tall posts send energy upward and create a strong wood vibration.

A sunrise alarm clock stimulates a natural sunrise by slowly getting brighter and brighter within a 30 minute time frame. This allows you to wake up naturally, rather than being jolted awake.

Eastern light

If you are building a house and have a say as to where the bedrooms are positioned, consider facing your house to the south so the bedrooms are in the northeast-east corner. The body is better rested when it wakes up naturally. You can achieve this by placing your bed so that you can see the sunrise without the light falling directly on the bed. Waking up under the full light of the sun can get hot and uncomfortable at certain times of the year.

WATER VIBRATION. Beds with a water vibration, such as a sleigh bed, promote relaxation and release. Any bed with flowing or curving lines will help you let go of what you picked up today that you do not want to carry into tomorrow. Wicker headboards allow air to flow through and promote a water vibration. (Actual waterbeds are not advised however, since the water in them is usually chemically treated and is rarely replaced often enough to prevent stagnant chi.

Bedroom lighting

Choose lighting that complements your skin tone and shows off your body. Not many people have a body that can withstand the scrutiny of harsh daylight, so remember this when you are thinking about how many windows you want and what type of window treatments you are going to have displayed.

Use diffused, soft lighting in the bedroom to complement your skin appearance, as well as assist in relaxing your body.

METAL VIBRATION. Metal beds pull energy into the center, and are best suited for someone needing to gather their energy at the end of a stressful day. Sales people, therapists, or anyone who sends energy out in many directions during the day can benefit from the focusing effect of a metal bed. Many metal beds do not have a solid headboard, however. Weigh the benefits of the metal with the lack of solid support behind your head.

For the most relaxing situation, this bed is as far from the door as possible and behind the midline of the room. The closet doors on the left and the bathroom door on the right remain shut when not in use. The only solid wall is behind the head of the bed.

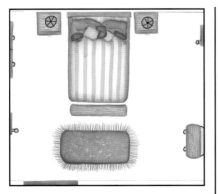

If you have to place the bed in the mouth of chi, use a rug or a hope chest at the foot of the bed to buffer chi. Keep the bathroom, closet, and main door closed.

Place your bed with care

Place your bed in the room before anything else. Since most bedrooms are limited in possible placements, use the following prioritized list to avoid stressful situations.

Proximity to the door. Place the bed as far away from the door as possible and behind the midline of the room. If the door opens right onto the bed, chi from the rest of the house tends to rush in too quickly, making it difficult to settle down and fall asleep.

Adjustments: If it is not possible to get the bed away from the door, have a solid footboard and close the bedroom door an hour before bedtime to slow the flow of chi. You can also lessen the energy by placing a rug or chest in between the bed and the door.

If you have a window behind your bed, create the illusion of a wall with drapes.

A solid wall behind your head. Since energy travels more quickly through a window than through a solid wall, windows behind your head facilitate the transfer of your energy to the outside world. If you tend to get colds often or fatigue easily, support your immune system with a solid wall behind your head.

 Adjustment: If you have to have a window at your head, be certain to use a solid headboard and place a pillow upright between your head and the headboard.

The metaphor of the nest works well in a bedroom where the couple nests in the shelter of one another.

Whether the bed is placed on a diagonal or against the wall, be careful not to stack things directly over the headboard.

Placing the bed at a diagonal. Avoid placing your bed on a diagonal. This creates a chasm directly behind your head, which greatly reduces how safe and supported you will feel in the bed. It also creates a more active chi flow in the room.

Adjustment: If a diagonal placement is necessary because of ceiling beams or the shape of the room, be certain to fill the empty space with plants or a folding screen. Visually filling in the space will increase the sense that you are supported.

Because the only option for this bed was a diagonal placement, the upshooting plant behind the headboard keeps the chi from stagnating behind the bed.

If an exercise bike is the first thing you see when you wake up, it is either a reminder of what you are not doing or an invitation to fulfill your needs for intimacy through a workout.

Coordinating items around the bed

The first thing you see in the morning will affect the energy you carry with you throughout the day. If you wake up looking at the toilet seat in the bathroom, imagine the effect that has on your day. If you first see your desk, chances are you will have a harder time separating from work. If it is a laundry pile you see, you will tend to focus on mundane tasks.

Overcrowding the bedroom

A common design error is over-crowding the bedroom. Sometimes this overcrowding comes with the addition of an exercise bike or desk, but sometimes it is the result of buying oversized, imposing bedroom furniture. Your furniture should fit the space you are currently living in. Do not fall into the trap of thinking "We'll buy this big furniture now because some day we'll have a real master suite." This creates a dissonance between your current reality and a hoped-for reality. Create balance, harmony, and flow in your life today, and future realities become a mute point.

Your bed should not be more than $\frac{1}{3}$ the size of the room, and all your furnishings together should not take up more than half of the total space. Energy needs to flow easily through a bedroom for you to relax. This also means not storing items under the bed.

Overdoing it in a bedroom makes it difficult to rest and relax. Keep things simple here.

Use a battery-operated clock to reduce the EMF impact of an electric clock/radio.

Electronics by the bed. Electronics emit strong electromagnetic fields (EMFs) that artificially stimulate the body. The body has a natural EMF that aligns with the sun's. Man-made EMFs are much stronger and oscillate, moving back and forth through the body at up to 50 herz per second. It is difficult, if not impossible, to completely avoid EMFs throughout the day. Computers, refrigerators, and vacuum cleaners emit strong EMFs and are a part of every day reality. However, with some simple adjustments you can create an EMF-free zone in the bedroom. Spending those hours during which your body is most vulnerable and most receptive to its environment in an EMF-free zone can have astonishing benefits, including a more passionate sex life.

Covering as well as unplugging a television set when not in use will reduce EMF stimulation while the body is trying to relax.

A covered bedroom mirror will reduce the energy bouncing through the room, allowing a more peaceful sleep.

Mirrors in the bedroom

Mirrors in the bedroom keep energy active and make it more difficult to settle down and rest in the space. If you think this energy bouncing back and forth all night does not effect you, try an experiment. Cover the mirror with a thick drape each night for a week and leave it draped while you sleep. Use this week to see if you sleep more soundly and deeply when the mirror is covered. If you find this helps, use one of the following adjustments to buffer your body from the mirror at night.

If your partner wants to keep passion alive by keeping mirrors in the bedroom, use one of the following ideas to permanently buffer your body from active mirror chi at night.

▲ If the mirror is large and attached to the wall, use a folding screen positioned across the mirror in the evening. This way you can have full access to the mirror when you want it, but not worry about it otherwise.

▲ Consider a fabric panel or a pull drape that hangs from a tension rod. The fabric panel can be pulled to the side much like a window treatment during the day, but can cover the mirror at night. A pull drape can be attached to most any surface and can turn your mirror into a hidden delight.

▲ If your mirrors are on the front of closets opposite the bed, an easy and beautiful treatment is to have a glass company apply a white tint to your mirror. The white tint will actually turn the mirror opaque and you will not have as much energy bouncing around.

▲ If the mirror is on a stand, simply turn the mirror to face the wall while you are sleeping or drape a piece of fabric over it.

Energy attaches to moving water. If the toilet lid is left up, energy continually drains out of the house.

Taking worry out of bathrooms

Bathrooms have received a lot of bad press in feng shui books, most of which does not apply to the modern bathroom at all. In ancient times, there was no plumbing and bathrooms were such a smelly place that they were constructed as separate buildings from the house (a Chinese version of the outhouse). You definitely would not feel like eating a meal, cooking, or sleeping next to the kind of stench that was associated with the bathroom. Modern bathrooms do not have these same problems, but there are still some energy dynamics that you will want to be aware of.

The purpose of a bathroom is rejuvenation and release. We renew ourselves and get ready to meet each new day in the bathroom. We also let go of everything that our bodies no longer need there. Bathroom design should enhance these two functions.

After an intense argument or exchange of energy with another person, when you feel agitation or turmoil in your body, just standing under the shower head and letting hot water run down over your body is healing and restorative. Water acts as a magnet to draw toxic emotions out of your body, leaving you feeling renewed.

Many feng shui observations view the downward force of running water as a negative thing. Energy attaches itself to whatever has the most density, and water is more dense than air. Therefore, energy will attach itself to water and fall into a pattern of following the water down the pipes and away from your house. If too much energy leaves your house, it can cause a drain on the overall health and financial resources of the house.

The problem is, once the pattern is established, it continues until something breaks the pattern. Therefore, energy will continue to flow down and away even if the water is no longer running, until you break the pattern. Just putting down your toilet lid or closing the drain in your tub is enough to shift the flow of energy. You are directing it to stay rather than leave. Although too much downward flow is not healthy, the downward pull of running water helps the physical body release more than just dirt particles. It can pull positive ions off the body, which is a tremendous help in letting go of stress. It can also enhance the body's ability to release and let go of the energetic charge that accompanies certain emotions.

Baths can rejuvenate when you use bath salts or orange rinds to draw toxins out of your body. Orange rinds are known for their ability to help you release sorrow.

- What time does my body usually want to wake up without an alarm? (the wake-up zone)

  _____

- When do I feel the most productive? (the work zone)

  _____

- When do I want to be around other people? (the social zone)

  _____

- When am I most likely to relax? (the relaxation zone)

  _____

- When do my creative juices start flowing? (the creativity zone)

  _____

- I sleep best between the hours of _____ and _____. (renewal zone)

Feng shui zones

The zone approach to feng shui is a method of taking into account how your personal biological clock and tendencies interface with the natural rhythms of the sun's 24-hour cycle. Individuals respond differently to the sun's signals of when to sleep and when to rise. Design books tend to assume that everyone rises with the sun, is active until about 3 or 4 P.M., slows down in the evening, goes to sleep at 10 P.M., and sleeps through the night. If that were true, however, sleep agents would not be the third most commonly sold over-the-counter drugs. Have you ever met someone who did not wake up until 11 A.M., got going around 4 P.M., and was fully functional around 9 P.M.? Don't you think this person would want to set his house up differently than someone who got up with the sun and was in bed by 9 P.M.? To understand your personal timing, answer the questions in the outside column on this page and fill in the Time-zone wheel, then read the definitions of each zone on the facing page. After that, you will be ready to make some adjustments to where things are located, based on how your clock is ticking.

Time-zone wheel

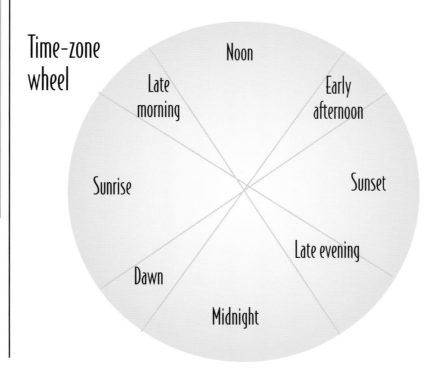

When your cycle is out of sync

The Time-zone wheel on page 278 will help you understand whether or not your personal time zones are out of sync with the sun's. If they are, you will need to use your environment to help you create the kind of energy for each zone that the sun normally creates during that time of the day.

12:00 NOON–6:00 P.M. (Fire to Earth)

Yang reaches its zenith during this stage, the transformational time of Fire. This Fire phase is related to the social zone. If you are not particularly social in the middle of the day, you will need something other than the sun to melt your boundaries and intensify your connections. After about 3 P.M., the yang begins to wither, slowly decreasing. As it decreases, it moves into an Earth phase again, the transitional element between yin and yang. If you never got revved up in the first place, this gradually sinking chi will leave you flat and lacking energy. Because this is an Earth time (around 4 P.M.), you will be tempted to reach for snacks of an Earth nature, including sweets, carbohydrates, and starches. This will further deplete your yang.

6:00 A.M.–12:00 NOON (Wood to Fire)

This phase is related to the wake-up zone and the work zone. During this phase, Wood energy takes root in the yin earth and uses the energy patterns of expansion, movement, and change to slowly increase yang. If you sleep until noon, you have missed the sun's increasingly yang acceleration and must provide that momentum for yourself. Waking up at a different time can leave you feeling tired all day long.

6:00 P.M.–12:00 MIDNIGHT (Earth to Metal)

Earth's density leads to Metal's contraction, allowing the earth's energy to be drawn back into a central core. This is a time of increasing yin. This phase relates to the relaxation zone and the creativity zone. Although the nature of creativity and relaxation depends upon the individual's primary element (a Fire person needs different things to relax than a Metal person), in general, this time of day is pulling inward, contracting, and refining. The sun sinks, the temperature cools off, and the earth's chi gradually becomes more yin. If you go to sleep before midnight, you can take advantage of the earth's increasing yin, which allows you to reach a deeper state of relaxation. If you do not go to sleep until after midnight, you are fighting the entire planet's momentum, as the next phase begins a gradual return to yang.

12:00 MIDNIGHT–6:00 A.M. (Metal to Water)

Metal's contraction brings the chi to a still point deep within. This deep stillness is Water's time to replenish chi reservoirs and restore tissues. Rising too much before 6 A.M. short-circuits the body's restoration process and can weaken the immune system. If your renewal zone does not fall between midnight and 6 A.M., you reduce the body's ability to hold Water chi, making deep restful sleep more and more of a novelty. (This applies even if you wake up during this time and then go back to sleep.)

The wake-up zone

This zone is an area in your home where you prepare to meet your day. The purpose of this space is to ease you into your day so that the transition from being asleep (yin) to forging ahead with full steam (yang) is made with grace and gentleness. Oftentimes, this area is your bed, a bathroom, or a breakfast nook. The function of this space is a limbo land—a place where nothing is expected from you and you can gather whatever forces you need to move into a more active phase.

Looking at your Time-zone wheel, pinpoint when you wake up. The traditional time associated with this zone is early in the morning, between 6 A.M. and 9 A.M. If your wake-up time differs, adjust for that difference by creating a place of transition in your home.

Your wake-up zone should help you transition from a state of complete relaxation to a state of intense activity.

280

The transition from Water to Wood. This transition is the most trying on the body and needs to happen gradually. Use Earth energy to support yourself while moving from a Water state of deep sleep to a Wood state of full activity. Earth energy is about holding chi, not moving it. You need a place that will physically hold you, such as your bed, a bathtub, or a deep comfy chair.

The lighting should be dimmed and localized. Try to avoid bright or diffused lighting. Just as your muscles are warming up, your eyes need a gradual transition as well.

Place your wake-up zone near a heat outlet or sunny window. During this state, your body has digested everything you ate the day before and is at its lowest biological temperature. If the sun is already up and streaming through a window when you wake up, great. If not, make certain that your wake-up zone is near a heat vent or that there is a blanket nearby.

Keep surfaces soft. A couch or pillowed nook works better for this zone than hard blunt surfaces. After a sleep cycle, your aura is more vulnerable than at other times of the day and you will be more affected by sharp surfaces.

Give yourself a chunk of time. Allow yourself five minutes to an hour in which you require absolutely nothing of yourself. Your ability to sleep deeply and relax will be greatly enhanced if your body knows it has a period of non-doing when it first wakes up.

281

Do not mix your wake-up zone and work zone. If you select a space for your wake-up zone that also holds reminders of all the things you need to get done that day, you will be tempted to give up this invaluable time in order to move on to something more "productive." This is why you should not put your office in your bedroom.

Adding pillows to this metal daybed softens it and increases its ability to support the owner's vulnerability.

The work zone

Your work zone should motivate and inspire you to action. Whether it is an office, a kitchen, or a garden, this area is where your productive, action-oriented self gets to shine. This zone is not about relaxing, taking it easy, or socializing. It is about manifesting in the physical realm whatever ideas, thoughts, or desires were generated during the relaxation and renewal stages.

Inspire yourself. A work zone needs avenues of inspiration. The link between the fantasy world and reality, a work zone needs links to the realm of imagination and spirit so that you do not lose sight entirely of why you are doing all this work in the first place. By adding a small fountain, a picture of a stream, or some other Water symbol, you can keep your Wood nourished and your projects flourishing.

Gather your tools together. Identify the tools of your trade and do your best to gather them all together into one workspace. Do you need a computer, kitchen sink, art supplies, internet connection, or stereo to do your work? If so, how many different rooms in your house do you need to access in order to have access to all your supplies? Reorganize cupboards, drawers, or countertops so that your work supplies are in one place. From this desk the owner can access:

- ▪ computer,
- ▪ phone and phone message pad,
- ▪ schedule and day planner,
- ▪ office supplies,
- ▪ garbage (underneath),
- ▪ fax machine,
- ▪ filing drawers.

The social zone

The social zone recognizes that we are all interdependent and participating in numerous communities at any given time. Just as we need places to be alone, we need places that facilitate coming together. How and when we choose to be together in community varies considerably. Looking at your Time-zone wheel, identify your best social hours. The earth's Fire phase is between 12 noon and 3 P.M. If that is your time and you are normally at work then, make certain your workplace has enjoyable coworkers or that you take the time to go out to lunch with your friends. If you are an evening socializer, modern society is set up to help you, since most social interactions occur in the evening after the workday. If you like company first thing in the morning, consider an early-morning walking partner or join a morning rowing club. If you tend to socialize after most people have gone to bed, your social space will need elements (such as a built-in bar or large-screen TV) that support nocturnal activities.

A cold passageway was transformed into a delightful sun room off the kitchen. Adding this room gave the owner a casual social zone in addition to the more formal living room.

Anything that captivates and delights the senses increases the sociability of a space.

The social zone is a Fire area. Fire energy represents the ability to let go of boundaries and inhibitions, connecting with others in an intimate, open way. Fire energy is stimulated by the senses. Therefore, the more senses you can activate in your social area, the easier it will be for people to open up there. Do you have a sound system? Is there food or drink available? Are the furnishings tactile? Does it smell good? Can you see beautiful, interesting, or stimulating things? Are there living things, such as animals or flowers in full bloom? Anything that activates the senses will enhance this area.

Curve your furniture to bring your guests together. Seating areas turned slightly toward each other, but not directly facing each other, allow guests to relax. Seats directly facing each other without furniture (such as an ottoman or coffee table) in between tend to feel confrontational and confining, rather than inviting.

Use lighting to set the mood. Increase intimacy in social settings by lowering the lights. The brighter the lights, the more exposed and vulnerable people feel, especially when getting to know a stranger. Lamplighting is especially helpful, because people gravitate toward pools of light. A few well-placed lamps can draw in even those individuals who tend to hang out on the periphery of social events.

The curved shape of this couch helps guests open up and converse with each other.

The relaxation zone

A time for relaxation can occur at any time during the daily cycle, from first thing in the morning to late at night. More than time of day, the five elements are more helpful in understanding what a person needs from the environment to "let it all go." For example, a Fire-energy person needs Fire energy in order to relax, which may take the form of alcohol or other stimulants. A Metal-energy person can only relax after cleaning up and getting everything ready for the next day. If you do not know your primary element, read through each of the following paragraphs and see which one describes you most, then set up your relaxation zone accordingly.

Nothing is more relaxing than water. Even a picture of a stream, the ocean shore, or a waterfall can induce relaxation.

This daybed works during the day, when sunlight is streaming in through the window. If you tend to relax at night, however, when the window is dark and the metal frame is cool, this spot is not for you.

How Metal energy relaxes. If you tend to relax in the evening, you might be a Metal-energy type. Since Metal constricts and pulls energy in, it might seem strange to think that Metal energy can help you relax. However, constricting energy is only part of Metal's role. Metal is also the sorting, distilling pattern that allows you to organize, make sense of, and place into meaningful categories, all the various events of the day. Without Metal's tendency to analyze, you would not know which parts of the day were the most meaningful to you or on which interactions you wanted to follow up. To help Metal relax, place cleaning supplies or organizing tools (such as list-making or planner entries) in your relaxation zone. For you, a few minutes of evening organizing or cleaning can clear the way for a deeper state of relaxation.

288

Arranging items on her bulletin board is a favorite relaxer for this Metal-energy client.

How Earth energy relaxes. If late afternoon to early evening is your time of day to let go, you might be an Earth-energy type. An Earth-energy person needs grounding in order to function. This means that Earth cannot relax until it first establishes a strong enough grounding that the person can let go of the many energies that build up in the aura like static cling on clothing. If you have a lot of Earth energy, your grounding cord is your way of letting go of anything that no longer serves you. Your form of grounding might be walking the dog, watering the grass, gardening, cooking, reading the newspaper, or swinging on a porch bench. Identify what activities help you ground and place the items needed for those activities in your home's relaxation zone. For example, hanging your dog's leash or your gardening gloves where you will see them every day will increase your grounding and support your need to relax.

A hammock or porch swing is a great way to relax. With your feet up off the floor, you will not be as tempted to jump up and attend to things as you would otherwise.

How Water energy relaxes. Can you only let go late at night when everyone else is in bed? Water energy might be your guiding force. Using the force of gravity, Water's flowing energy gradually slows and sinks until it reaches a point of absolute stillness. It is in this deep still place that Water finds the spiritual connection and resonance it needs to make sense out of the day's events. Once connected to the inner realm, external events become understandable and tolerable. Without this internal connection, it becomes increasingly difficult for a Water-energy person to relax. Rushing water is not the key here, rather slow-flowing chi and stillness will serve you better. Therefore, select a small fountain, a journal, or a meditation cushion to find your way inward, and make certain your relaxation zone has dark, not light, colors.

A quiet corner to sit in is usually all that Water requires to relax.

How Fire energy relaxes. Associated with the heat of noonday and the intensity of summer, Fire energy requires constant stimulation. Because of this need, Fire-energy people tend to be easily addicted, turning to smoking, alcohol, shopping, or sensual pleasures to raise the Fire in their bodies to a high enough level that they can "relax." Fire craves the experience of transcendence, escaping the limitations of self and merging with another person's energy field. To fulfill this need, Fire-energy types are often "touchy" people, giving others a hug or a brush on the arm, because contact reassures them and helps them feel safe. To experience the mundane or the ordinary feels like a trap that could snuff out their very life force. The key for Fire is to find ways to experience the beautiful, the extraordinary, and the sensational within the mundane ordinary world in which we all live. To be caught up and transfixed in a beautiful play of rain against your window or the smell of lavender on your sheets can satisfy Fire's passion without excess or destruction. Your relaxation zone needs sensual stimuli and connection with others (such as a cozy place to snuggle on the couch). Only then will you feel safe enough to truly relax.

Beauty has the power to seduce Fire into a relaxed state.

How Wood energy relaxes. Seem to keep going all day long? You are probably a Wood-energy type. Relaxed Wood energy might seem like an oxymoron, since Wood is the energy related to action and movement, but even Wood needs to relax. Most Wood-energy people continue to go until they drop, using utter fatigue or sickness to help them relax. If you want to be able to relax without getting sick, you need to coax your Wood into

- Allow for brief pauses, time-outs, in which you utterly let go of whatever project you are working on.
- Ten-minute power naps are a favorite Wood-energy break, as are stretches you can do at your desk.
- Try standing up and touching your toes between phone calls or giving yourself a neck or finger massage.
- Another Wood relaxant is learning how to do just one thing at a time.

Since Wood is accustomed to juggling five things at once, slowing down enough to do just one thing, such as drive the car (without picking up the cell phone, eating lunch, or jotting down notes), is a huge move forward in the relaxation department. Identify one place in which you commit yourself to do only one thing at a time. This area will function as your relaxation zone.

The creative zone

Want a place in your home that jump-starts your creative energy and gets your juices flowing? Like the relaxation zone, the creative zone is determined primarily by the elemental typing of the person. Often associated with the Metal element (just one type of creative expression), creativity means connecting with what the Taoists call the *Tao* or "Source." It is the life-force energy that runs through us and encompasses us at all times. By connecting with that life force, we can better understand how our gifts express and give shape to that force. Creativity is our expression of Source that stems from our unique experience of it. To understand what type of space might inspire your creative offerings, read on.

Earth energy gets creative. The primal mother figure, Earth expresses life force by nurturing and caretaking others. Earth energy is most creative when coming up with ways to care for and support others. You know your Earth energy is at work when you find yourself doing things for others that you would not do for yourself, such as making your neighbors a nice dinner or sewing elaborate Halloween costumes for your children. Your creative zone might be your kitchen, your sewing room, your garage, your dinner table, or your living-room sofa. Wherever you find yourself artistically expressing the desire to care for others, you have discovered Earth's creative zone.

Making something from Mother Earth, such as this wreath, will nurture Earth energy's creative side.

Water energy gets creative. Water is the depths of our being, our still point, and our connection to realms beyond the earthly realm. Therefore, Water's creativity strives to touch the core of a person and offer a glimpse of things that lie beyond the self. Water creativity has some challenging aspects, though. For example, you cannot rush Water's deep insights or force Water to compromise its message for the sake of a director's whims or budget. Integrity, honesty, and self-sacrifice are Water's trademarks, as many a starving artist can attest. To support your creative Water energy, give yourself long periods of uninterrupted silence. Close the door, unplug the phone, or leave town. Do whatever it takes to free yourself from the constraints of the physical world in order to open to the mystical and divine.

Metal energy gets creative. Metal energy is intellectual, verbal, and analytical in nature. Metal gets creative by forming unique combinations of words, thoughts, or ideas. These combinations might be expressed in written form, through conversation over dinner, or as a computer program. However Metal chooses to express its creative force, it tends to use symbols and systems, rather than Earth energy's acts of kindness. Metal tends to look for a laboratory, a computer, or a classroom in which to create. If it cannot find one of these spaces, it will tidy up and create order in whatever space it finds itself. Organizing is Metal's way of bringing abstract systems and patterns into the physical realm.

A quiet and solitary place to sit and journal draws Water energy's creativity to the surface.

Wood energy gets creative. Wood energy thinks best on its feet. Fast and sure-footed, Wood does not understand why Water needs so much time to do everything. Decisions are made instantaneously and changed just as fast. Time is of the essence and productivity, not morality, is the highest value. Not to say that Wood energy is immoral. It simply finds no enjoyment in verification and paperwork, rather it delights in the discovery of something new.

Wood-energy people are the pioneers—those adventurous souls who dare to try something that has never been done before. To support your Wood, you simply need to get out of the way. Do not slow it down with long-range planning or conditions, let it grow unimpeded. If you are a Wood person, fill your creativity zone with the tools you need to embody your ideas in form, regardless of whether that form is a product, a paragraph, or a corporation. One caution, however. You love the creative stage, but hate to complete things. Find a way to pass your creations on to someone else who will bring them to completion or surround yourself with Metal energy that can help you finish what you start.

Fire energy gets creative. A sight, a sound, a taste, or a touch is all Fire needs to open into creative expression. Feeling stymied? Get a playmate or a pet. Creativity and play are one and the same for Fire energy and nothing will help you feel more creative than a person or pet who will play with you. Therefore, fill your creativity zone with all kinds of toys—a new motorcycle, a stunning CD collection, a blooming Christmas cactus—and invite others over to play.

With bright colors, fresh flowers, munchies, and all kinds of games, this room is set up to encourage playfulness in guests of all ages. Whether it is for a midnight snack or an evening of movie watching, Fire enjoys inviting others over to play.

The renewal zone

Some individuals sleep best if they get to bed before 9 P.M.; others need to stay up until at least 11 P.M. in order to avoid a restless night. Your sleep style is an important consideration when setting up your renewal zone. If you tend to sleep in late, you will want blackout shades to keep the sunlight at bay. If you wake up before dawn, especially in the winter, you might want to add a sunrise alarm clock to slowly brighten the room. Even if you sleep a regular eight hours from 10 P.M. to 6 A.M., be certain to keep the following in mind:

Renewal is a Water-energy state. For this reason, standing under a hot shower can be as invigorating as six hours of sleep. If you have a difficult time getting to sleep, take a hot bath right before bedtime or deepen your sleep rhythm by adding the sound of running water in your room.

Avoid patterns. Renewal is a yin state. Solid colors are more yin in nature, whereas patterns are yang. Busy active patterns in your bedding can influence you even after the lights go out, since you hold the visual memory of the pattern in your head.

Use dark colors. Dark, subdued colors, such as black and dark blue, generate Water energy and help people achieve a deeper, more restful sleep. Try a week of midnight-blue sheets followed by a week of white sheets and see which ones help you sleep better.

New sunrise alarm clocks help you rise before dawn without aid of natural light. All have simulated dawn light. Some feature white noise to block out traffic and other unwanted sounds.

The neutral color scheme in this bedroom is restful and promotes healthful sleep. The red pillow, which adds a bit of passion, is easily thrown off the bed when it is time to sleep.

A matter of light

Plan for a comfortable balance between natural and controlled light.

One of nature's strongest yang forces, lighting affects everything else in the room. If the lighting is too diffused, for example, it prevents the eye from focusing easily on individual objects. This happens often with overhead florescent lights. On the other hand, lighting that is too dim generates a strong yin effect on the body, bringing on depression and dark moods. This chapter will focus on the following three factors to evaluate your home's lighting: color, illumination, and chi flow.

A floor filled with dappled sunlight recalls an intimate connection with the sun's force.

295

Light is one of the most powerful chi enhancers of all environmental elements. It represents consciousness and awareness. To understand something better is to "shed light on it," and to bring something "to light" means to become aware of its hidden, subconscious meanings. Light is also a powerful regulator of moods and physical body systems. To date, there have been more than 3,000 studies on the effects of light on human chronobiology (our internal rhythms and cycles activated or controlled by light.)

Color

Full-spectrum lighting. Full-spectrum lighting has received quite a bit of attention lately. Just about every major line of lightbulb manufacturer now produces a full-spectrum bulb. Just what is full-spectrum lighting good for? Full-spectrum lighting eliminates spikes in the color spectrum, thereby producing a more balanced white light. This means the colors you see in the items around you are true colors because the light itself is not absorbing more of one color ray than another. Your gold looks gold, not greenish gold, and your periwinkle wall is just that, periwinkle.

Why blue light might be better. As we age, the cornea hardens and yellows—everything we see gets more and more yellow. There are lightbulbs available now that adjust for the yellowing of the cornea and create a truer color representation. For anyone over the age of 60, lightbulbs with a blue bias are beneficial.

Color temperature. Another feature related to color is the temperature of the color ray. The Japanese have conducted research on the physiological responses to high and low color temperatures, and found that high color temperatures (the 5000–6000 Kelvin range) enlarge pupil size and allow more light to the retina. This means, with the right temperature light, you will need less illumination (See **Illumination** on page 297).

This hand-blown glass lighting fixture brings memories of a trip to Italy, as well as illumination, to this dining room.

Illumination

Illumination is most important in the winter when you do not get as much natural exposure to bright outdoor light. You need illumination, especially first thing in the morning, to keep your body's many chemical and emotional cycles in balance. One of the most documented imbalances caused by a lack of bright light is seasonal affective disorder (SAD). Discovered in 1980, SAD is triggered by the shorter daylight hours. The lack of light (illumination) allows the body's sleep signal, melatonin, to build up to higher than normal levels, which disrupts the body's daily sleep-wake cycle. When the sleep-wake cycle is disrupted, you feel the symptoms of jet lag:

- clinical sleep disorders,
- severe fatigue,
- major digestive problems,
- the inability to react or concentrate.

What is the best solution? As noted on the previous page, full-spectrum lighting produces a more balanced white light, but does nothing to increase lux (the amount of illumination). It is the lack of brightness, not the color of the light, that results in SAD. Additionally, you need that illumination at a particular time of day, especially early in the morning, because you have got to reset your internal clock. Your internal clock is a pair of very small organs in the brain called suprachaismatic nuclei (SCN). How it actually works is that the retina detects light, sends the signal to the pineal gland, then the pineal gland activates the SCN, which in turn tells the pineal gland to stop producing melatonin. That said, here are some effective measures for getting your biological clock back in sync.

A small reading lamp behind the couch adds much-needed light to this area during winter months.

- Light-boxes have been a highly recommended adjustment for SAD sufferers, however, they have limitations. For starters, you have to spend an hour every morning staring into a bright square of light (no wonder people try medication rather than spend their time this way). Also, some of the light-boxes do not have UV filters on them, which can damage the retina and skin.
- Light-visors have been proven just as effective as light-boxes, and do not require staring into a bright square of light for an hour every morning. The light does not need to be as bright because it is positioned closer to the retina. They also have UV filters.

Allow as much light as possible by opening your curtains and blinds, no matter which season reigns outdoors.

- I strongly recommend a simulated-dawn alarm clock (sometimes called a sunrise alarm clock), which simulates the sunrise and helps reset your body's internal clock.

- Resist the temptation to draw your curtains or blinds during winter months. Allow as much natural light in as possible.

- Get your windows cleaned regularly. A thin film of dirt can block up to 50 percent of your precious sunlight.

- Adjust your work schedule to allow for an hour outside every day during daylight hours (sunlight ranges from 10,000 to 100,000 lux, whereas a brightly lit office is only about 1,000 lux).

- If possible, add a skylight in an area of your home that does not receive as much natural light due to the lower placement of the sun in winter.

- Add incandescent lamps in rooms where you spend a lot of time.

This alarm clock simulates the rising sun, naturally awakening the body just as it finishes a rapid eye movement (REM) sleep cycle.

Using light to direct chi

Balanced light. Is balanced light a good thing? As mentioned earlier, when light becomes too diffused, i.e. too balanced, our ability to perceive individual objects diminishes. Diffused light also loses its ability to direct chi. In yin/yang theory, there must be places of darkness in order to comprehend places of light. Only through dimming areas of a room can other areas stand out. Allow for shadow, but use it artistically. Like the mat surrounding a well-framed painting, shadow can help you highlight a room's-defining characteristics.

Identify sources of natural light. Light is a design variable that changes throughout the day and with the seasons. In the winter, the sun sits lower in the sky than during the summer, and of course, southern exposures will always be brightest during the middle of the day. Once you know how much natural light you have in different areas, you will know better how to supplement it with artificial sources.

■ Identify the time of day you are most likely to be in a certain area (See **Feng shui zones** on pages 278–294 to work through this).

■ Watch how the light changes throughout the day. Supplement with task lighting.

■ Use window coverings that allow for variable lighting options.

■ Think about the function of the space and how much light you need to work there. Some functions, such as making crafts or cooking, require general lighting. Other tasks, such as reading or tying flies, need localized task lighting.

■ Once you know your needs, add task lighting in the form of lamps, spotlights, undercounter lights, or tracks for areas that support detailed work.

You can't have a light without a dark to stick it in.

—Arlo Guthrie

Localized task lighting for leisure reading is ideally placed near your favorite chair.

Use lighting to identify focal points. For rooms with more than one focal point, or rooms without a strong focal point, use a spotlight or row of track lights to draw the eye to your designated center. Wherever light is strongest, that is where the eye goes first; everything else is secondary.

Lights should move up as well as down. Since lighting directs chi, sometimes you will need to move energy up a wall, as well as down. For wall lighting, your eye will focus on the fixture and move from there. If the fixture directs light upward, your eye and your chi will rise. If the fixture directs the chi downward, your eye and your chi will sink.

300 **Consider using sconces like those pictured below, which direct light up as well as down, to balance the space.**

Intuition

Now that you have read an entire book to understand the principles that work in feng shui, it is important to stress the role of intuition in creating your living space. Intuition is a powerful sense of knowing whether something is right or not by connecting to a shared consciousness, an energetic force that transcends time and individual personalities. Many feng shui masters intentionally give their students conflicting advice to help them understand the power of intuition in reading the energy of a space.

What does intuition have to do with feng shui? Feng shui is a series of guidelines that work to put you in touch with your intuition, not replace it. Intuition is your permission to play. Try things out, see how they feel, and follow your intuition rather than rules. If the fountain feels better in the Family Heritage area of your home than it does in the Abundance area, trust that. Perhaps that familial relationship needs more nurturing than your pocketbook at that time of your life. When I consult with clients and explain to them the positive impact of good choices they have made in placing their furnishings, they often comment "it just felt good there."

As you make your feng shui adjustments, be certain to pay attention to how your body feels. If you feel queasy in your stomach, you should replace the placement. If you hang a picture, for example, and you realize that you are feeling more distant, cut off from the rest of the world, rethink that adjustment. On the other hand, if you move your grandmother's piano to a certain corner of the living room and the music sounds brighter and crisper than it did before, you know you have made a change for the better. Let your body be your best guide. And if it tells you to put a hammock in your living room, trust it.

About the author

Sharon's background in psychology led her to develop an approach to feng shui that reveals how one's deep psycho-logical patterns surface in one's external environment. Having worked with hospitals and healers of numerous disciplines, Sharon integrates Chinese medicine, traditional feng shui teachings, Jungian psychology, and shadow-therapy work into her feng shui consultations.

She delights in helping clients discover their purpose and align their lives to support that purpose. Sharon currently runs Self Start, a training center in Salt Lake City, Utah, that provides advanced business training and mentoring for feng shui consultants, professional organizers, and life coaches. Sharon balances her work life with two amazing boys and a joyful marriage.

Acknowlegements

Special thanks to the following artists and companies for sharing their exceptional products with our readers:

Pgs 17 & 191: Magda Jakocev–Ulrich, the Studio for Art, Architecture, and Interior Design

Pg 48 desk: Novikoff, Inc., Fort Worth, TX 800-780-0982 www.novikoff.com

Pg 153 bunkbed: Stanley Furniture, Stanleytown, VA 540-627-2000 www.stanleyfurniture.com

Pg 182 oval boxes: Charles Harvey

Pg 193 wooden chairs: Robert Sonday

Pg 198 desk: Century Furniture, Hickory, NC 828-326-8317 www.centuryfurniture.com

Pg 221 corner cupboard: Robert Wurster

Pg 268 Martha bed: Frewil, Inc. Los Angeles, CA www.frewil.com

Resources

SELF START, Inc. 703 E. 1700 S., Salt Lake City, UT 84105. Provides advanced business training and mentoring for feng shui consultants, professional organizers, and life coaches. Contact Sharon through her web site at www.selfstart.net, call 801-519-9161, or e-mail her at fstc@xmission.com.

The Feng Shui Training Center. Provides core training for feng shui practitioners. Contact them at www.thefengshuitrainingcenter.com, call 801-519-9161, or e-mail Sharon at fstc@xmission.com.

Clear & Simple. Provides the only professional organizer certification training program in the United States. They also provide organizing support for homes and businesses throughout the US. Reach them at clearsimple.com or call 801-463-9090.

Photo Credits

Michael Skarsten, Salt Lake City, UT: 78(t), 237

Jessie Walker, Glencoe, IL: 54(b), 55, 56(r), 57, 58(t), 59(t)(b), 64, 65(b), 66(t)(b), 67(t), 68, 70, 73(b), 78(b), 81(r), 82, 88(tr), 92(b)(tr), 93, 96, 97, 98(t), 100–101, 106(t)(b), 107(t)(b), 108, 109,(t)(b), 112, 113, 114–119, 120, 122, 123, 124, 128, 129, 131, 133, 136, 137, 139, 140(t), 141, 225(b), 226(bl), 227(br), 228(b), 229(tl), 232–233, 238(r), 240(b), 242(cl), 246, 247, 249(t)(l), 250, 281, 292, 293, 294(b), 298(t)

Scott Zimmerman, Scott Zimmerman Photography & Kevin Dilley, Hazel Photography: 5–53, 146–205, 211–221, 252–277, 301

Artville (©1997): 72

Corbis (©2000): 58, 104(tr)(b), 125, 126, 244(tr)(b), 284(l), 287(b), 288(r), 289(t), 295(r)

PhotoDisc (©1995, 1999, 2000, 2001): 68, 73, 76(tl)(bl), 81(l), 89, 95(bl)(br), 98(r), 103, 110(b), 127, 143(tr), 145(r)(l), 227(cr), 232(ct)(br), 234, 239, 242(t)(c), 280(tl), 284, 286(tr)(br), 287, 287(t), 290, 291, 295(l), 299

Index